CHRISTIAN PRESENCE
IN THE
NEIGHBORHOOD

Christian Presence in the Neighborhood

by PIERRE TALEC

Translated by
NELS CHALLE

"Behold, he has come to
proclaim peace, a peace
for those who are far
and for those who are
near."

(Eph. 2, 17)

NEWMAN PRESS

Westminster, Md.   New York, N. Y.   Glen Rock, N. J.

Amsterdam   Toronto

A Newman Press Edition, originally published under the title *Initiation à la Mission,* Casterman, 1965. Copyright © Casterman, 1965.

Library of Congress
Catalog Card Number: 67-23601

Published by Newman Press
Editorial Office: 304 W. 58th St., N.Y., N.Y. 10019
Business Office: Westminster, Maryland 21157

Printed and bound in the
United States of America

CONTENTS

6 *Contents*

FOREWORD

A certain number of lay people, engaged in what we at Saint-Severin call the "neighborhood mission," want to involve themselves in missionary activity. They have felt the need of acquiring a formation that will allow them to act with discernment and competence. This present work is a summary of a course especially prepared for their needs. It is the echo of a parochial community anxious to find a mode of Christian presence in the neighborhood.

In a large sense, this work is addressed to all Christians who are called to live in truth the responsibilities of their baptism; it proposes to help all those men and women who question the world in which they live and the mission of the Church in our days.

This study does not pretend to be an exhaustive work on the subject of missionary theology. Nor is it a discourse on missionary methods. Seeing the light of theology while hearing the cry of the world, mine is an essay of reflection. It is presented in didactic form to permit Christians to order their knowledge and coordinate the elements for their judgment. It is the expression of the Church in a state of council.

How can we implement the great options of the universal Church contained in Schema 13 if we do not study what are the tenets and goals of the mission?

What are the contents of the mission? Beyond diverse methods of action, what are the constructive elements of every missionary act? What is the foundation of the mission's demands? To whom does the mission address itself? Who is responsible for it?

How do we enter into contact with the men of our times? How do we initiate dialogue? Can the Christian engaged in the structures of the city hope to have some missionary effectiveness? What is the worth of Christian institutions? What are the missionary possibilities in the parish?

Such are the questions raised by Vatican Council II. Looking

7

ahead, they are questions we ask ourselves about tomorrow's world.

Will the technological world find priests working in that world?

How does the Church foresee the evangelization of the world of leisure?

These are open questions, the study of which is still going on.

PIERRE TALEC
Curate of Saint-Severin

I

IN THE LIGHT OF THEOLOGY
The Contents of the Mission

1 THE PROBLEM
The Christian and Today's Mission

1. Foundation of the Missionary Duty

The "mission"—that active concern which must excite Christians in the world of unbelief—is the means by which Christians express the evangelical necessity of illumination which Christ summed up in very simple images: "You are the light of the world. . . . Let your light so shine before men in order that they may see your good works and give glory to your Father in heaven (Mt. 5, 14. 16).

The Christian is essentially one who radiates. The life of the Christian is a harvest; he returns a hundredfold what has been sown in him. The life of a Christian is a perpetual opening-out. All that he receives, he passes on. This law of fruitfulness is inherent in the very nature of his being from the moment of baptism.

By the sacraments of baptism and confirmation, the Christian becomes a participant in the love of God. Because the love of God, of its very essence, is shared, the Christian can adopt it only through communicating it. The mission is nothing else than the movement of exchanging, by which we share the heritage that we have received from Christ. Faith is a gift of God; it is a talent to render fruitful. A man cannot live in faith and content himself with being sheltered by God in a fidelity that is only interior. If it is not transmitted, the faith of a Christian disintegrates before dying. Many Christians accuse themselves of losing their faith, but one does not lose faith if he gives it to others.

There is no need, I think, of further justifying the necessity of the missionary responsibility. Since it imposes itself as a basic exigency of the sacraments of baptism and confirmation, why bother appealing to sentiment or psychology? Must we use an arrray of statistics to make an impression? Finally, it is of little importance to us to know the proportion of Christians actually

11

inscribed on our baptismal registers. What compels us is, as St. Paul says, the love of Christ. Let us ignore every missionary statistic; if there were only one unbeliever in the world, it would be reason enough for all of us to give up our lives to make Christ known to him.

2. The Missionary Temperament

The methods of translating our missionary duty into action seem as confused as the necessity appears clear. How do we make personal the Church's mission? To what does the mission correspond concretely? Is the mission possible? What are the exact contents of the word "mission"?

Many Christians have tried for generations to "carry on the apostolate" (according to the consecrated expression). Considering the impasses encountered in many so-called apostolic efforts and the pious advice and inefficiency of so many missionary attempts, these Christians want to have a clear heart. Is missionary activity within the reach of the average layman, who perhaps may not have the vocation and character of a declared militant of Catholic Action? Must the priest in his parish, who may not have the vocation of a priest-worker or apostle to underdeveloped nations or a missionary to South America, look for situations of extraordinary ministry in order to attempt missionary work? Do priests or lay people today have a missionary opportunity in the "traditional" Church?

When we hear certain priests and laymen belittle their aspirations, we have the impression that the best Christians compensate for their inability to act in a really missionary way by an expenditure of energy in the blind activism of parish activity. Thus, in the parishes the grand illusion is created that everything has become mission-oriented, because from the Mass to parish carnivals every activity is "baptized" as missionary—a baptism that unfortunately does not correspond to that of desire. Christians seek consolation by persuading themselves that everybody is doing what he can.

When we question ourselves honestly about the profound and immediate reasons why the mission has bogged down, we should admit that we are undertaking a path as narrow as it is perilous. Only the loving fidelity of those who suffer for, and because of, the

Church can assure our march forward in all loyalty and fairness. Every searching Christian is led into making a judgment about the past, the present and the future. In so doing he risks taking his personal intuitions for the inspirations of the Holy Spirit and posing as an apostle of his own mission.

Considering the present situation of the Church according to criteria which implicate people and institutions, he runs the risk of being misunderstood. Will not the reflection he makes be interpreted as an unkind criticism? Even in the name of charity, he will be suspected of ill will. He will be called upon to give his proofs: "Physician, heal thyself." Let him show what he can do!

In these impasses where he finds himself enclosed with the others, isn't the poor missionary volunteer as unequipped as any other? Has he the liberty or the leisure, beyond these one-way streets, to take advantage of the experiences that seem opportune to him? No one can be a prophet of the mission without being somewhat the martyr. Before involving ourselves as volunteers, we should know what missionary action will cost. Humanly and supernaturally speaking, a certain number of qualities of a moral and intellectual order are required:

(a) *To have the courage of the wrestler who has no fear of danger.* The apostle, according to St. Paul, is he who puts up a good fight and for whom the words of the Lord are confirmed: "I am sending you forth like sheep in the midst of wolves" (Mt. 10, 16).

(b) *To be sufficiently detached from our good works to know when to discard formerly useful practices that have now become outdated.* Too many Christians remain attached to respectable activities that have aided the devout people who pursued them but that do not give satisfaction on the missionary level.

(c) *To know when to accept a temporary pause in the action in order to safeguard liberty of judgment and lucidity.* We should destroy only in order to build. Is it necessary that the rubble of the past be an obstacle to every new construction project? Should we maintain a still-smoldering wick, yet leave the whole light under the bushel-basket? In other words, should we content ourselves with attitudes of preserving and temporizing? Does the inability to adopt effective measures on the spot justify maintaining mediocrity?

(d) *To act with competence.* The mission is not the product of improvisation, just as good literature is not produced with good sentiments alone. Can the Christian mission be "made" with sentiments that are not always good? We know that the kingdom of God is of the supernatural order. Is this any reason for us to imagine that we can operate as amateurs? It is not the role of grace to compensate for human foolishness. Many setbacks in the work of building the kingdom of God could be avoided if men did not attribute to the cross what should be attributed to their own errors. We have to acquire a missionary technique, a missionary intelligence and a missionary heart.

3. Those to Whom the Mission Is Directed

(a) *Use of the Word "Mission."* Words too often lose their meaning. Some have become nothing but words. The word "mission" has not escaped that tendency. It is used at random and often misinterpreted to indicate realities at very different levels. An article misplaced or the order of the words is sufficient to give the word "mission" a very different sense. If General de Gaulle had to speak of mission, he would speak of the mission of France, and obviously there would be no connection with the "Mission de France" indicated in the work of Père Godin, *France, Pays de Mission.*

For most people, the word "mission" evokes, above all, exotic and picturesque images. When the word "missionary" is spoken, a certain number of clichés impose themselves upon the imagination: the white habit of the bearded man holding a bare-bottomed little black African by the hand, the large, menacing lions, the canoe on a bamboo-bordered river, as well as the gold candy-wrappers sent to the missions for the little black children (paper already emptied of their chocolates by little white children), the canceled stamps, the used magazines, the special collections, etc. All of that is certainly a part of the mission, but it is not *the* mission. The present term "mission" seems to be more and more free of all geographic implication. Let us try to extract its essential contents.

(b) *The Difficulty of a Definition: Mission—Pastoral—Pastoral Mission.* In a wide sense the term "mission" designates the action of the Church directed toward those outside, as opposed to the term "pastoral," which designates the action of the Church directed toward those within.

Categories

Those within can be divided into three *categories:*

1. Those who are called true Christians—that is, those who live their faith in an enlightened way. These are the good practicing Christians.

2. Those who are called "sociological Christians" and who live their Christianity in a traditional and customary way—for example, the regular attendants at wakes and funerals and the practicing formalists known as "Sunday Christians."

3. Those who are called the sick in faith and who range from neurotic mystics, through the superstitious, to the bigots. These are the false believers, practitioners of religion who find in Christianity something to feed their sickness.

Those "outside," in the strictest sense of the term, are the pagans (from the Latin word *paganus,* rural-dweller). The word flourished in the 4th century, the era in which St. Martin was evangelizing the isolated countryside. In a larger sense, pagans are all those who do not know Christ. St. Paul calls them the Gentiles (from the Latin word *gentiles,* inhabitants of nations which have not received the message). Pagans may be religious or atheistic. Religious pagans worship idols; they do not refuse God. The atheists reject God and even the idea of God. They are, in general, either the agnostics who deny all possibility of the knowledge of God, or the militants of an adverse ideology—the Marxists, for example. Among atheists can be found the believers who have rejected their faith; these are the turncoats. There are also numerous unbelievers who are so because of indifference.

In addition, there are the false believers. These are either unbelievers who don't believe because they picture faith according to the caricatures which they establish and create themselves, or else they are unbelievers who basically have faith, but who prefer, for the sake of a clear conscience, to refuse it intellectually rather than to live it.

Those outside together with those inside: the *pastoral* mission. This third distinction attempts to correct the caricature of the first two (which schematize reality by simplifying it) and to reconcile them. The *pastoral* mission is the action of the Church directed toward those within with the same preoccupation we have for those outside. It is addressed to:

(a) those whom we have called true Christians, that they might organize to take over those outside;

(b) the sociological Christians who are inside but who act as if they were outside. The *pastoral mission* attempts to bring them to conversion.

(c) those outside, but with methods suitable for those within. For example, at Saint-Severin the "neighborhood mission" corresponds to this form of pastoral action. It is an effort to be present to the world bounded by parish limits. If this effort to reach the neighborhood is crowned with so little success, it is because the neighborhood has been approached as if its people were already "those within."

Do we believe that our parishes and our movements can reach people who are totally indifferent to what is familiar to us but so foreign to them? Have we tried to realize what unbelievers might think of all the works that we perform to win their favor? How do they judge these activities which, from our point of view, are missionary? These works undoubtedly have the value of contact, sympathy and witness. But what disproportion exists between the inherent limitations of what we are now doing and the urgent needs of the unbelieving world. All too often, unbelievers view our snack-times for elderly people, our nurseries, our guilds with the reaction: "So the Christians make a specialty of good works! So what?" *Inside* methods employed for those *outside* are met with thoughts such as these: "What are these women doing, busying themselves in this way? They are obviously ladies from secure families who have nothing to do at home. What are all these priests doing amusing children? They have to do something and they have no real work to do. They have to take care of other people's children because they have none of their own to raise. So much the better; they are helping us. We can use priests; they are good fellows, our benefactors."

From the witness of charity which we priests and lay people attempt to give, what value can be drawn? Is it the proclamation of Jesus Christ? Is it the call to conversion? It is all well and good to adapt our means of making Christ present, to modernize and renew our methods, to appear liberal, but such actions are only preliminary.

This *pastoral* work deserves its qualification as "missionary" by reason of the solicitude that it manifests for those outside; it deserves the name "pastoral" because of the peace it engenders in many Christians who do not set limits to their generosity.

Mode of Action of the Pastoral Mission

The *pastoral* mission is based on the value of acceptance and openness. It strains itself to make the house pleasant so that the unbeliever who looks in from outside may view an agreeable interior. It is the threshold mission. The unbeliever does not enter; the believer does not go out. But the utmost is done to provoke sympathetic contacts; attempts are made to understand one another, to believe in dialogue, to establish unity if only on the surface. This *prepastoral mission* cannot be taken for the true mission. Of itself it is like those water lilies blooming at the surface of a stagnant pond. From the strictly missionary point of view, the Christian must go out to breathe the air of the world which insults him to his face, and be an envoy to that world.

Possibilities and Limits of the Pastoral Mission

This pastoral mission offers the advantage of making us aware of the complexity of the object of the mission. The world cannot be reduced to schematic categories: the good and the bad, the saved and the damned, believers and unbelievers. In each man may be found all the soils of which the parable of the sower speaks. Therefore we must look for a method of raising the grain through the broken stones and undulations of the terrain. The pastoral mission which addresses itself to "outside" people with "inside" methods has the disadvantage of wanting to reconcile everything;

as a result of its flexibility, it lacks character. Wishing to stimulate the believers, very often it only passes most of its time with the false believers; wishing to meet the unbeliever, it does not go beyond the limits of the false unbelievers. It vegetates in half-measures; it lacks energy.

4. Conclusion

Overwhelmed by the immediate and urgent tasks in this terrain plagued by thorns and weeds, we tend to content ourselves with simply clipping instead of uprooting and planting. We have lost our concern for those who do not really know Christ; we no longer even know how to recognize them in our Christian civilization where all the realities of the world are viewed through the illusion of Christian folklore and art which give the impression of a non-pagan world.

Let us not delude ourselves about our *pastoral* mission. Let us act so that our good sentiments may not hide from us the hardness of the world of unbelief. May the impasses not trap us in impossible dilemmas! In effect, the layman entering into contact with the world fears making himself the accomplice of what he condemns, and he asks himself honestly what must be done: to be a missionary of the Gospel or to resign from the world? The priest, obliged by his office to do many works that have no missionary value, asks himself: "Must I be condemned to missionary inefficacy? Must I be either priest *or* missionary?" This is the temptation to which he must not succumb, and he would not succumb if it were not nourished by the sin of the laity's inertia.

2 THE "WHY" OF THE MISSION
The World's Vocation: The Church

If, before the world, the Church looks at herself in the mirror of the Gospel, it is because she wishes to present herself in a manner agreeable to men of her times. If the Church questions herself, it is not to question the contents of her faith, but rather to judge her own comportment with respect to the world. She asks herself how she can communicate the message she must reveal.

Since the Church must enter into sympathetic rapport with the world, we are naturally led first of all to question the world itself, to consider it with its needs and adequacies, its aspirations and rejections and contradictions. This wish to understand the world is an attitude imposed as an indispensable preamble to the dialogue. To know in order to understand is the way of good sense and logic; and yet, it is the way which we deliberately do not take, for there is another logic: that of revelation.

We cannot approach the mission using human establishments as our point of departure. To visualize the mission uniquely in terms of these establishments is to reduce the richness of the message of salvation to the world's capacity to receive it. This message is transcendent; it comes from God and goes far beyond anything that the world might desire. The role of the mission is to make the world discover what it should desire. The world cannot be approached in the manner of a general who remains on the defensive, knowing his battlefield in terms of the troops he commands. The mission must climb and forge ahead. It must attack, first of all, because the world is hard: "You will be persecuted. Be sly like serpents. . . ." But, above all, it must attack because by nature the Church precedes the world, and the world's role is to permit the Church to carry it along.

I

FUNDAMENTAL IDEAS OF THEOLOGY

Having acquired a certain human wisdom, we should disengage ourselves from our human point of view to discover the wisdom of God and adopt his point of view. We should see the world as God sees it. To approach the world, not in terms of any lucidity we might have, but in the light of God, is to pass from the anthropological point of view, which we naturally have toward everything, to the theocentric point of view. For the Christian, this means questioning the world not from what he sees, but from what God reveals to us in the scriptures.

It is hardly necessary to stress the fact that this goes against our most natural tendency. We are in the world. Psychologically, we examine what counts for us. We therefore have to make a certain effort in order to adopt this theocentric point of view. But it is only from this point of view that we can demonstrate what we must affirm. For God, and consequently for us, what is primary in existence, in the reality of things, is not the world but the Church.

1. The Preexistence of the Church Rests on the Primacy of Christ

The fact of the creation of the world and of its origins is revealed to us in the Book of Genesis: "In the beginning, God created heaven and earth." The finality of that creation is explained to us by the New Testament, in particular by St. John and St. Paul. "In the beginning was the Word. Everything was created by him and *for him*. He is the head of the body which is the Church. For God pleased himself by making live in him all plenitude, and in reconciling all beings for him."

All the mystery of the Church is contained in the creative plan of God summed up in Christ. The mission of the Church is itself contained in this plan. If God drew out of nothingness all those beings whom he created, it was for Christ; and since Christ is the Church, it might be said that he commanded creation for the Church. As a matter of fact, if we really believe in the primacy of Christ and recognize this identification of Christ with the Church, where is the difficulty in admitting the preexistence of the Church in the world?

In the order of existence—we might say chronological existence —the Church appears before the world. She precedes the world. True to holy scripture, all tradition affirms it. The Church was created by God before all things. "Do not believe," said Origen, "that the Church has existed only since the coming of the savior in the flesh; she has existed since the beginning of mankind and even since the creation of the world. (I refer to St. Paul as authority here.) The first foundations of the Church were therefore laid from the beginning. That is why the apostle also said that the Church is founded not only on the apostles but on the prophets, and Adam himself is counted in the number of the prophets." [1]

Those of us who have remained at the elementary level of our childhood catechisms will no doubt be astonished at this affirmation. Didn't we learn at catechism that the Church was founded at Pentecost? Pentecost is the historic moment *par excellence* of the existence of the Church. The event of Pentecost makes us discover that, in the essential order, the Church has existed forever and will exist forever. "From the Church as well as from Christ, it must be declared that his kingdom will have no end. The wedding of the Lamb will be eternal." [2]

To be sure, the appearance of the Church, as we see her today, will pass with the changing world, but in the reality of the mystery which she contains, the Church will have no end. At the beginning was the Church. At the end will be the Church. Like Christ, whom she proclaims and prolongs, she is the alpha and the omega. She is part of the eternal realities; she rises out of eternity to appear in time. She carries the world at her breast. She enters its heart to remind it: "It is I who gave birth to you; if you live, it is through me; it is for me."

The Church at Pentecost is instituted visibly, constituted in power, confirmed and formed in the paschal mystery. At Pentecost, the Church is born. Like a fiancée promised to her spouse for a long time, she is given to the world. She receives, we might say, her investiture. She receives, at the same time, her mission. She takes wing and manifests herself. This manifestation is precisely the

[1] Cited from H. de Lubac, *Meditation sur l'Eglise*, p. 51.
[2] *Ibid.*, p. 53.

mission. The mission is the fecundity of the Church communicating herself; it is the revelation of the mystery of the Church who, founded invisibly from all eternity, unveils herself and her reason for being on earth: to wed the world made for her, to call men to be her children. Here, then, is the double mystery of the Church —wife and mother.

At the heart of the mystery of God there is the Church; at the heart of the mystery of the Church there is the world. Between the world and the Church there is a bond of reciprocity which unites them as in a home where the parents and children complete each other. Just as the child has need of his parents to live and the parents have need of the child to give their home fullness and completion, so does the world have need of the Church—its mother—to live, and the Church has need of the world—her child—for her growth and fulfillment.[3]

But it is not the world which enlightens the Church; it is the Church which is the light of the world. To understand the world in the light of God, we must regard it through the light of the Church. This affirmation of the preexistence of the Church belongs among those facts which seem to go without saying from the point of view of faith, but which are too quickly forgotten when the reality of the world is perceived. And yet, it is squarely on this fact that the missionary theology of the Church and the world rests.

2. Corollary Affirmation: The Vocation of the World Is the Church

Often we hear it said that the Church's vocation is the world. This is not a false affirmation. Indeed, to the extent that the *raison d'être* of the Church is the world and to the extent that the Church must summon the world, from the necessity of overture and reception it can be deduced that the vocation of the Church is the world. But it is not because the Church's *raison d'être* is the world that her *mission,* as well, is the world. It is said that God calls men to his love (creation is the proof of that love); we do not thereby deduce that the vocation of God is man. It is the very opposite which must be affirmed: the vocation of man is God.

To say that the Church calls the world does not mean that the

[3] Cf. M.-D. Chenu, *La Parole de Dieu II,* pp. 299-300.

fulfillment of the Church is the world. It is uniquely because the Church's function is to summon the world that it can be said the vocation of the Church is the world. This expression is thus employed in the sense of causality. But since the fulfillment of the world is to realize itself in the Church, it is clear that it is not a game of words to affirm in the plan of finality that the vocation of the world is the Church.

A writing of the primitive Church entitled *The Shepherd of Hermas* attempts to make us understand this change of perspective. The creative vocation of God was actualized in the creation of the world. The world is the actualization of the creative will of God, and the Church, married to the world, is the realization of God's intention to give the world the quality of a world redeemed. Since intention precedes will, the Church truly precedes the world. That is what, in substance, *The Shepherd of Hermas* said: "Just as the will of God is an act and this act summons the world, the purpose of God is the salvation of men, and this purpose is called the Church." [4] This distinction between purpose and will is equivalent to the one we have made on the philosophical level between finality and causality.

From the God-centered perspective which we have adopted, it becomes clear that it is the Church which must first be known, so that the mission, conforming to what the Church is, can faithfully rejoin the world as it is. What is your sense of the Church? What is your love of the Church? No mission is possible without a thorough understanding of the mystery of the Church. To understand the problems of the world, the mystery of the Church must be explored. We must know how to recognize in the Church the world which we wish to know in life. It is only in this perspective that we will be qualified to lay hold of the fulfillment of the world revealed in the bible through the sense of creation.

3. The Missionary Structure of the Church

The term *ecclesia,* which comes from the Greek, expresses the totality of the mystery of the Church. She is at the same time *convocatio, vocatio* and *congregatio:* an answer to the call which is made in the assembly. *Convocatio,* the call of the Church, is not

[4] H. de Lubac, *op. cit.,* p. 53.

an optional invitation; it is a convocation. The world, to be faithful to what is within itself, must respond to that convocation or it cannot become what it must be. That convocation is collective; it is not addressed to men taken separately and understood in their personal relation to God. It is addressed to man in his social dimension, living in relation with other people.

The Church convokes all the world, the good and the bad. She convokes to assemble. The Church in the world is a little like the schoolmaster on the playground who calls all his pupils to reunite them in one class, the physical and spiritual place for their growth. Since this appeal contains in itself the means of responding, the Church is at the same time the source and the resting place of this appeal, the means of salvation and salvation itself. To the extent that she holds the means of salvation, the Church presents herself to men as the institution of salvation, with her visible signs, her exigencies and her conditions. To the extent that she realizes the end which she proposes, the Church is already the communion of grace toward which men strive and which makes of all men in-corporated in Christ one body, the Church invisible.

Visible Church and invisible Church: these are the two insepa-rable faces of the same mystery which must always be regarded together, at the risk of bending the mission unilaterally in one direction or the other. The rapport between these fundamental ideas of theology and our missionary research is of primary impor-tance, because the way in which we envisage the mission reflects our grasp of the mystery of the Church in its entirety.

From the 17th to the 19th centuries, the thoroughness of theo-logical research is reflected in the evolution of concepts. After the Council of Trent in the 16th century, the stream of theology begin-ning with Bellarmine was strongly influenced by the Counter-Ref-ormation. At the moment when Protestants were contesting the rights of the pope and the Church, Rome had but one concern: to consolidate the institutional Church and to safeguard the hier-archical Church. Mission could therefore not be conceived of without giving primacy to the visible Church. Mission became the function of the institutional Church.

That mission consisted of giving to men the possibility of using the Church, in her hierarchical and sacramental organization, as the means of salvation. To be a missionary was essentially to work to make men enter the fold. It was during that epoch that the expression, "There is no salvation outside the Church," became current. The risks inherent in this tendency are clearly visible: to consider the limits of the institution as absolute, while minimizing the reality of the invisible Church which assembles all mankind in the communion of grace for the same salvation.

Surely to refuse the means instituted by Christ is to refuse the incarnation and to put oneself outside the normal means of salvation. But on the other hand, to make the institution the only criterion would be to commit the equally serious error of those who would reduce the mystery of the Church to invisible realities. The theology of the end of the 19th century, in giving the institution its proper emphasis, should have complemented this by placing an accent on the mystery of the Church as the community of grace. The stream of theology issuing from Mersch has contributed toward orienting the mission in the direction of an appeal to all men, energized by the divine love in them, to participate in that sign of the Church which is already realized in the communion of all men united in Christ.

This fashion of viewing the mission has the advantage of shedding light on the most profound aspect of the mystery: to identify the community of grace. But if it isolates that community of grace from the means of salvation of the visible Church, it presents the risk of conceiving the mission in a disembodied manner. A well-balanced theology will be clearly aware of the two aspects. The role of mission is to put the world in the state of grace and thereby participate in the life of the body of Christ. The mission realizes that state of grace through the signs of the visible body: the sacraments and one's relation to a single community faithful to the Church.

II

THE MISSIONARY IMPLICATION

1. Mission and Adaptation to the World

The Church, which precedes the world in the order of creation, goes out to meet the world in order to wed it. This statement should not be taken to mean that the Church must change. The Church, which participates in the eternal mystery of God, does not change. It is precisely for this reason that, in the face of an ephemeral world, she has the words of eternal life.

What is meant by the Church's adaptation to the world? There is obviously some disparity between the world's appearance and the mask worn by the Church for the world. The concept of adaptation is tied up with that of change. He who adapts himself must develop as a function of the one who remains the same. He changes to conform to the model, which does not change. Since the Church is eternal, the world must adapt to her. The precise role of the mission is to permit the world to adapt itself: to become what it should be.

But the world will be able to accomplish this conversion only if the Church decides to abandon her clown makeup and costumes so that the world can recognize in her the unwrinkled, unblemished spouse. When we speak of the adjustment of the Church to the world, we mean simply that the Church, in the formulation of her needs and the presentation of her message, must be aware of mental evolution, of the world's requirements, of the scandal of the weak, of scientific and theological progress. She must give up that style of life impeding dialogue with a world which judges the mystery of the Church by the signs she displays.

Finally, to say that the Church must adjust to the world means that she must act as teacher to the world. The world is the raw material of the Church. The Church—the yeast in the dough— must give it shape. Rephrasing what H. Desroches has said, the Christian missionary task is to know simultaneously how the Church will be the form of the world and how the world will be the material of the Church.[5]

2. Faith and Mission of the Church

Our faith in the Church, which precedes the world, should fill us with strength and not timidity. Too many Christians approach the world with fear. We must go into the world convinced that the message we carry has at least as much value as the worldly cus-

[5] M.-D. Chenu, "L'Evangile dans le temps," in *La Parole de Dieu* II, p. 299.

toms competing with it. Often, under the pretext of tolerance, the Christian gives up on the uncompromising Gospel message and pretends to be a freethinker. If the Christian really believes that the world is made for the Church, he should have no fear of revealing to the unbeliever the fact that the Church concerns him, whether he likes it or not.

It is evident that the Christian, faced with the transcendence of the message he must carry, should make this revelation with the humility of one who offers his own possession but reveals it as something belonging equally to the unbeliever. The Christian does not pretend to present the truth; he does not pretend to present Jesus Christ, because he who is truth is already present in the world.

3. The Church's Youth

Since in the order of theological precedence, the Church comes before the world, she should not follow a course of adaptation that is in any way posterior to the world. In this respect she should take the initiative and be creative. Sadly enough, however, she has known a history of considerable delay in this regard. When she has taken steps to reform, she has found herself faced with the task of updating things on which she has long delayed. Consequently, she begins much further back, relatively speaking, than the world in her course of adaptation. It can hardly be termed a revolution in anticipation when the pope decides to terminate the Royal Guard three centuries after the Renaissance. The Church will have to adapt by anticipating, and it falls to Christians to see beforehand the evolution taking place in the world in order to be prepared to baptize what emerges from it. Far from being pretentious, this is consequent upon what we have demonstrated theologically, namely, that the Church precedes the world.

4. The Mission Proceeds from Love

This desire to precede the world admittedly risks degenerating into an attitude of dominating triumphalism. This results in forgetting that the Church's mission arises from love.

Because God loves the world, he sent his only Son. Because the Church loves the world, she goes to meet it, not to dictate to it but to guide it, knowing how to stand aside like a good guide.

The best way of revealing the Church's mission of summoning the world is to let the Church's humility show through. This humility is rooted in the fact that the Church does not seek her own glory, but rather acts as a messenger to the world, just as Christ was the messenger of the Father. If the Church acts like a servant, it is not part of an act, but rather because her mission is to serve the world as Christ served it. This attitude eliminates the fraudulent aspects of the mission: proselytism, triumphalism, paternalism, etc.

5. The Mission Is Universal Because the Church Is Catholic

The poverty of the Church is, paradoxically, the wealth which will persuade the world that the Church calls all men. It is an old temptation for the Church to limit her appeal to an elite few who are capable of responding to her and of making her look good. But the Church, which participates in the holiness of Christ and is therefore the source of holiness, is the sinners' Church. The Church should not succumb to the temptation to regard herself as a haven of saints when viewing this so convincingly sinful world. The choice between the masses and the elite presents a false dilemma. The Church does not have to choose between the masses and the elite. She summons the masses through the elite.

The Church's work cannot be done in an individual way, limiting the proclamation of the Good News to isolated people, for the Gospel is rendered ineffectual if it is addressed anonymously to compact masses. The role of the mission is to arouse the elite and split them up, thereby reducing the masses to human-sized communities where the relationship between the masses and the elite is that of a living cell.

6. The Mission and Awareness of Salvation

All men are saved. Christians are those who know it; the others do not. The mission consists of making known what God has done to save all men. It also helps to make people be what they should be: intelligent beings who know who they are. It is the mark of the intelligent man that he calls things by their name; the mark of the Christian is that he calls God "Father." The mission is to reveal.

7. Mission: The Church Visible and Invisible

How can we remain faithful to both the visible and invisible aspects of the church? We have seen that the institutional Church is the enclosure necessary for the life of the flock. The institutional Church is willed by Christ. The enclosure may be soiled by sin or reeking with scandal, but denial of the fact is no solution. The Church cannot be denied because there is sin within her unless at the same time one denies the grace of the Church. The missionary should not give the impression that only those who are in the enclosure can be Christians. Neither should he let it be thought that men of goodwill, whatever their belief, finally find God in the same way as they would in the enclosure. Yes, all men are saved, but the Christian will gain salvation in the way that God wishes to save all of us.

In concluding this reflection on the mission of the Church facing the world, we might compare the mission to a river flowing to the sea. The Church is the source, with the world at its mouth; the role of the mission is that of the current, sweeping it along. Springing up from the source, the mission enters into the world, mixing with it. But while the river is lost in the sea, the mission allows the world to find itself in the Church.

3 THE ACTORS OF THE MISSION
One Baptism: Laity and Priests with the Bishop

If a certain discomfort is noticed when priests and lay people work together, it is often because the foundations of the functions and rights of each are not known. We cannot approach the question of the laity without at the same time considering that of the priesthood, and vice versa, for they throw light on each other mutually.

I

THE THEOLOGICAL FOUNDATION
OF THE PRIEST-LAITY DISTINCTION

The priest-laity distinction rests upon the very structure of the Church: the body of Christ composed of a head and members. "For as the body is one and has many members, and all the members, many as they are, form one body, so also is it with Christ. For in one Spirit we were all baptized into one body" (1 Cor. 12, 12-13). "Again, he is the head of his body, the Church" (Col. 1, 18).

"You are the body of Christ, each one with his own function." *Each one with his own function:* there's the problem. What is the function of each one? The choice of our condition of life is not absolute; it depends upon our personal vocation. The difficulty in grasping what is specifically lay or priestly is caused by the fact that often the two vocations encroach upon each other. Lay people behave in a clerical manner and priests live as though they were of the world. We must recognize who we are and what role we must play in the body of Christ, the Church.

Christian existence is different for each Christian according to the way he is bound to Christ. His way of belonging to Christ

31

could be called his state of life. And each Christian can assume this way of belonging to Christ only in connection with the relation of Christ to all men. Christ, in his relation with men, presents himself in the three characters of his incarnation, as priest, king and prophet. The Church, which prolongs the incarnation of Christ, was instituted by Jesus himself to ensure these three functions: priestly, royal and prophetic.

To find our role in the body of Christ, we must first know what these three functions really involve and how lay people and priests live them. We start by looking at them in Christ himself.

1. *Christ the Priest:* As priest, Christ is mediator between God and men. Only he can ensure the sanctification of all humanity. He is consecrated to bring to the Father all creation, which he assumes in the person of the Son of God and which he offers in the sacrifice of his life. The Church, offering through the liturgy, assumes to herself the sanctifying worship of Christ the priest. This is the priestly function of the Church.

2. *Christ the King:* As king, Christ leads with power and authority all men whom the Father draws to him. In this sense, Christ is a shepherd. The Church, which leads men toward the Father, assumes this royal or pastoral function through him who is the only true shepherd.

3. *Christ the Prophet:* As prophet, Christ is the only true witness of the Father. He reveals the Father to us; no one could know the Father as well as the Son. The Church, in preaching the Gospel of salvation to all men, proclaims the message through those who are responsible for keeping the revealed trust. This is the prophetic function of the Church.

These three vital functions of the Church are taken up variously by Christians according to their vocation in the body of Christ. How must priests and lay people respectively take up these three functions? We are all members of the body; Christ alone is the head. But since the ascension, Christ, as head of the Church, has transmitted his powers to certain members who, while still remaining only members, yet carry out the vital functions of the head.

From this we see that some are exclusively members; these are the lay people. Others are at the head; these are the bishops and the priests. The problem now is this: Are those at the head of the Church *exclusively* so, or can they at the same time be simple members?

This distinction is not drawn from psychological criteria, according to a leaning toward a particular kind of life, but rather in terms of the *character* which marks each one in the body of Christ. Therefore, we must examine the specific character of the sacraments of baptism, confirmation and holy orders.

II

DISTINGUISHING THE ROLE EACH ONE MUST PLAY

Baptism is the sacrament which makes all those who believe in Christ members of the Church. At the same time that it bestows upon the Christian the grace of belonging organically to Christ, it expresses that grace by a distinctive sign, an indelible mark, called a character. The baptismal character shapes the Christian and makes him like Christ the priest, rendering him a principal participant in his priesthood and, consequently, in his kingdom, in his prophetic role.

Since he participates in the priesthood of Christ, the baptized person enters, in the broad sense of the term, into the hierarchy to which he belongs. The baptismal character consecrates the Christian organically into the body of Christ and prepares him to exercise his role as an active member of that body. The Christian receives this grace in fullness through confirmation. This sacrament expresses the grace of strength which it imparts through its own character. The confirmation character adds its specific mark in that it shapes the baptized person, already likened to Christ the priest, to Christ as he exercises his royalty and his role as prophet.

The sacrament of holy orders endows the baptized and confirmed person with the grace of leadership, which Christ possesses in perfection as head of the Church. This important grace is also expressed by a distinctive sign: the priestly character. This priestly character reshapes the baptized person, already participating in the priesthood of Christ, to Christ the priest in his role as head of the Church. The priest takes part in the priesthood of Christ as a member who has the power to transmit the grace of Christ the leader.

Just as baptism is fully completed by confirmation, so does the priesthood attain its fullness in the episcopate. The power of transmitting the grace of Christ the leader belongs in abundance to the bishop, who receives from Christ the governing authority to lead the flock. This power of governing makes the bishop a member of the "hierarchy," in the modern sense of the term. It is upon this hierarchical power that the apostolic authority of the bishop is founded. The word "hierarchy" comes from two Greek words: *hieros,* sacred, and *arche,* principal or leader.

We have seen how the baptized person belongs to the hierarchy. As a participant in the priesthood of Christ, he benefits from the priestly grace of Christ which on certain occasions confers upon him the power to exercise the priesthood of Christ. Baptized persons are the ministers of the sacrament of marriage; they can also baptize. In this sense, they participate in the power of the hierarchical order. But the modern sense of the word "hierarchy" is reserved for the power of apostolic authority, which may be exercised only by the pope and bishops. In this sense the hierarchy consists of the assembly of bishops, successors of the apostles, grouped into one single episcopal body, with the pope as their head. Since they were commanded by Christ to lead the flock, they have received for this mission the power to nourish the flock. The hierarchy thus defined constitutes the teaching (magisterial) Church. Since priests are in charge of passing on Christian teaching to the baptized, they join with the bishops in the function of the teaching Church.

The priest is an assistant in the pastoral mission of the bishop. In Canon Law he is called "priest of the second rank," in the sense that he only participates in the complete priesthood of the bishop. The bishop has the primary responsibility for the mission in accordance with the desire of Christ. It was to his apostles that he gave his powers, and not to just any follower. The recitals of the appearances of the risen Christ agree on the fact that it was to the apostles that he said: "Go into the whole world and preach the Gospel to every creature" (Mk. 16, 15).

The lay person, as opposed to the bishop and his co-worker the priest, is defined as one of God's people, considered formally distinct from the hierarchy. The etymological sense of the term "lay" comes from the Greek *laos,* people, from which is derived the adjective, *laikos,* of the people. The common denominator of priest-laity can be more clearly seen now: priests and lay people belonging by their baptismal character to the same priestly, royal and prophetic race. The lay people act as members, whereas bishops and priests act as members functioning like the head. The body of Christ lives only by the cohesion of the head and the members.

III
DIFFERENCE IN MISSION
ACCORDING TO PRIESTLY AND LAY VOCATIONS

The lay person receives the grace of baptism and confirmation in order to exercise his role of an inside member of Christ's Church and to fulfill his Christian mission. He does not receive the special powers by which bishops and priests exercise the three functions of the Church: order, at the priestly level; jurisdiction, at the royal or pastoral level; and magistracy, at the prophetic level.

The Priestly Duty of Priest and Layman

The priest, through the sacerdotal character with which he is marked when he receives the powers of holy orders, is likened to Christ the priest to the extent of being called *"alter Christus,"* another Christ. Consecrated to the Church's service, he is, for the People of God, the sacramental Christ who transmits life. He offers the liturgical sacrifice of God's people *in persona Christi,* which means not as a simple delegate of the faithful but in the name of Christ, whom the priest represents for the faithful. As mediator between God and man, he is truly the *celebrant* of the mysteries.

The priest, when he celebrates the eucharist, constitutes the Church by that very act. The bishop, ordaining new priests and anointing new bishops, makes the Church present in her hierarchical establishment. There is a great difference between the members of the body of Christ, who participate in the life of the body by making it function, and the head who communicates life to the body in giving it birth. It was with this thought in mind that Yves Congar wrote: "The priestly acts of the faithful are in the realm of the liturgical actions which express the Church but do not constitute her."

The lay person, as a member of God's priestly people, is entitled to divine worship. He offers, he communicates, he gives thanks. The baptized person is really the actor of the liturgy, the sacrament of his priesthood. It must be emphasized that he carries out this priesthood of the baptized through visible ecclesiastical acts and not through a piety which arises from private devotion. This priesthood is spiritual and interior; it should not be confused with the functional and hierarchical priesthood of the priest. But that does not mean the layman's priesthood is inferior. Stated briefly, the lay person is author of the celebration under the title of participant, whereas the priest is author under the title of celebrant. It should be specified that this nuance between the participating layman and the celebrating priest in no way minimizes the value of the baptized person's interior offering. The priest recalls this fact several times during the Mass, when he invites the congregation to pray to the Lord with him.

The Royal or Pastoral Function of Priest and Layman

Here is the function *par excellence* of the missionary action. The priest is, before all else, an initiator. Receiving the bishop's instructions, he assumes them, passes them on and adapts them to the concrete situations in which he finds himself. His role is one of instruction, advice and impetus. He enlightens the judgment of the engaged militants by giving them the means of judging by the light of the Gospel. He guides the revision of life and tries to enlist more militants from the ranks of stronger Christians. He is careful not to minimize the value of traditional works, showing those fit for them the necessity of engagement in these structures. For those who work within the traditional structures, the role of the priest is to bring out the missionary point of view in their action—a difficult task, for, as we have seen, the undeniable generosity of lay people often deludes them as to the missionary effectiveness of their activities.

The lay person is really responsible for the mission. These are not just idle words. He is responsible by virtue of his baptism and confirmation and as a participant of the eucharistic community. His participation at the eucharist gives him the duty of transmitting the sign of universal love which he receives.

To assume this responsibility, he must take the initiative. The very idea of responsibility implies initiative. For him, the initiative is a right. He can assume this responsibility in a privileged domain where the priest cannot: that of the temporal, of life. This is the layman's own domain, which gives him a superiority of action over the priest. The lay person, with regard to the teaching Church, may have the impression of being in a dependent situation, like a child with regard to his parents; but the ordained minister has this same impression regarding the world in which he lives, feeling like a child unable to assume responsibility in the city.

In building the kingdom of God in the *world,* the lay person assumes in his own arena that prerogative which is the priest's in building the kingdom of God in the hierarchical Church. The clergyman cannot be part of the world because of his way of life (he is not married, has no profession, does not earn a living, cannot take part politically, economically, socially, etc.). The lay person, however, builds the kingdom of God by his participation in the world, that is, by the contribution which he makes to the world's achievement through working in the cities of men.

The Christian in the world does not have the special sacramental powers of a priest, but he does have the power to enlist himself as a militant. It is this power, conferred by the sacraments of baptism and confirmation, which gives to the lay person his missionary character.

If we can permit ourselves this comparison, the priest has the role of dramatic director, whereas the lay person is the actor responsible for his acting, having full freedom to adapt it to the most diverse situations. Or, if the lay person is the yeast in the dough, it is the priest who watches over the quality of this yeast and the rising of the dough.

The Prophetic Function

Most simply and directly explained, the mission's role is to make Jesus Christ known; the prophetic function is to permit the realization of that proclamation. It is essentially a matter of talking of God in God's name. It is interesting to note that in the bible the prophet's vocation is defined as the mission. "I will send you to lead my people," Yahweh said to Moses (Exod. 3, 10). We find the same thought in Jeremiah 1, 7 and Ezekiel 2, 3; 3, 4. Priests are responsible for proclaiming the Word himself and for preaching the Word.

Priests and lay people are responsible for teaching. The catechesis is put to work in this prophetic function. Lay people living in the world are especially responsible for translating the Word into act. This translation is called "witness," and we will discuss it later.

Conclusion

The solidarity of the team of laity and priests should make us aware that the Church of Christ can live in the unity of his body only if each one of the organs fulfills the role which it must play. St. Augustine spoke of the clergy to his faithful: "With you, we are Christians; for you, we are bishops and priests." This underlines the fundamental unity of priests and lay people as organs of the same body, but at the same time it considers them in their proper relation to each other, for they are really bound together in the same Church. It is better to say, with Cardinal Suhard: "Not priests serving lay people, not lay people serving priests; rather, priests and lay people together serving the Church."

IV

THE DEPENDENT RELATION OF THE AUTONOMOUS LAY APOSTOLATE TO THE HIERARCHY

The layman's right to initiative in his missionary responsibilities is granted as a consequence of the baptismal character. By what right, then, can hierarchy give a mission or mandate to Catholic Action movements? What does the mission involve? In what name does it prepare Catholic Action for carrying out its mission?

The Hierarchy and the Laity: The Question of a Mandate

When the hierarchy intervenes, it is always in terms of the entire flock. Since it is responsible for the missionary orientation of the whole Church, it must judge the value and opportunities of apostolic methods and establish a choice among the different forms of action. Concerned for the good of all, its role is to coordinate the efforts of each in order to harmonize the efforts put forth from all parts. Considering the extremely varied situations in which the apostolate must act, it can establish special missions adapted to particular circumstances: for example, the Mission of France, the Mission of Paris, the Mission of the Sea, the Mission in the Latin Quarter developed at Saint-Severin, etc.

To adapt the mission to different environments which escape territorial bounds, the Church must be organized. The jurisdiction of bishops is confined to one place, to one diocese. But, according to the Council, bishops are bishops of the universal Church and of all who pass through their dioceses. This is why the hierarchy must not only take charge of apostolic organization on the territorial level of the diocese, but also relate the apostolate to differing environments.

The hierarchy has delegated this task of the organization of the environmental apostolate to Catholic Action, recognizing it officially as the mission to arouse and coordinate all efforts undertaken from the missionary point of view. This pastoral authority to govern is explained concretely by the *mandate* of Catholic Action —that is, by the apostolic mission it gives through the prerogatives which confer on it the apostolic power of responsibility for the mission as we have defined it.

The hierarchy does not give this apostolic mission to Christians taken individually. It is the sacrament of baptism which directly and rightfully bestows on every Christian his missionary responsibility. An assembly of cardinals and archbishops in 1946 declared explicitly: "The laity do not have to wait for a delegation of powers to fulfill their individual missions. It is enough for them to be faithful to the demands of their baptism and confirmation." Thus, the mandate adds nothing to, and removes nothing from, the mission conferred by baptism.

After the crises of the ACJF and the JEC, certain militants of Catholic Action considered the notion of mandate to be outdated and superfluous, and they contested with the hierarchy for the power of granting Catholic Action its apostolic mission. Without foundation they put the laity's right of initiative on the same level with the power of pastoral government properly belonging to the hierarchy as head of the flock.

This difficulty of comprehension, which has provoked the so-called *mandatory crises,* shows us clearly that the mission of Christians in the world is always a mission of the Church.

(a) *The lay person,* as an organ of the body of Christ, individually presents an incontestable missionary autonomy. But as a member of the flock, he can use his baptismal right of initiative only if he moves in the direction of the whole flock's mission. If he is irritated by receiving a mission of movement from the hierarchy, it is because he does not understand that the bishop always regards missionary action in terms of the entire flock for which he is responsible.

(b) *The bishop* does not command Christians to go on a mission; rather, it is the grace of their baptism which does this. The bishop calls them to move in conformity with the mission of the entire flock, in step with the Church.

This fundamental autonomy of each member of the Church, as well as the interdependent relations of all members, emphasizes the organic character of the mission inherent in the organic character of the body of Christ. "The Church," says Yves Congar, "is structured from above, but she also lives from below. She exists first of all through her clergy, that part of her which, as the depository of apostolicity of the ministry, visibly continues the works of Christ, generative of a community of faithful. But this role is played only when the community collaborates with its priests." [1]

Practical Consequences of Laity-Hierarchy Relations

Therefore, the mission, which gives hierarchy to Catholic Action in presenting it with an apostolic command, does not substitute what each baptized person receives through baptism and confirmation. The mandate is only a measure of a judicial nature which assures—on the pastoral level of the group for which the bishops are responsible—the right of initiative of the laity who, guided by the Holy Spirit, act as members responsible for their action.

However, some of the objections raised by certain militants of Catholic Action should be retained. These objections are revealing

[1] Cf. Y. Congar, *Lay People in the Church.* Fr. Congar, who makes the statement in another book, uses "celebrates" as a synonym of "collaboration."

as to the relations which should exist between lay people and bishops. According to these militants, the mandate is often an abuse of hierarchical power, substituted for the missionary power conferred by baptism. It is a way for the hierarchy to assume the authority possessed by the laity on the personal level. It has become the hierarchy's guardianship in its eagerness to control the laity and reduce lay initiative. It may be that certain objections are in fact justified, but not from the point of view of principle. The bishop in charge of the entire flock must avoid leading it like an army in which the men are not trusted. If lay people are treated like drafted soldiers, their right of initiative cannot be respected.

Bishops should not reduce the filial obedience which they expect from lay people to an utter lack of confrontation. It is possible that the mandate strengthens a certain authoritarian temptation of the hierarchy.

The dialogue should not be carried on in a unilateral fashion, priests and lay people together on one side, priests and bishops together on the other. It should be established at the laity-bishop level. Too often, lay people think they have to go through priests to reach the bishop. They should present their point of view directly. Priests, acting as intermediary diplomats, are liable to present the bishop with the lay people's problems reviewed and corrected according to the way they present their own questions.

It is up to the bishops to listen to the laity's point of view. But lay people must stop approaching the bishop as if he were a benign Buddha to be consulted on important occasions. They must disturb the bishops, report their difficulties and propose their projects. The truth in this human relationship will be the sign of their filial devotion. The layman should know that the missionary role of the bishop, shepherd of the flock, sometimes demands that he be a scapegoat.

4 THE MISSIONARY ACT
Proclamation of the Word

Well-meaning Christians, "wanting to do something," are often discouraged both by the vagueness of the tasks proposed to them and by an indecisive clergy. Not knowing what exactly is needed, we get lost in analyses, considerations and plans; we do nothing; we lack daring; we procrastinate with half-measures; we console ourselves with pious prayers; we are afraid of great undertakings.

Such uncertain conditions of action are discouraging. Disturbed by all sorts of criticism, the controversy raging on all sides and the incessant requestioning, the eager Christian may even give up completely. In this climate of doubt and uncertainty, it is important to keep our footing and to lean on the unshakable constants of action.

Beyond all forms of action and at the very heart of all missionary action, what criteria must be objectively referred to in order to avoid missionary pragmatism and verify the value of the action? What are the basic elements of every missionary act?

1. The Basic Elements of the Missionary Act

There is obviously no dogma which unalterably fixes the rules of missionary action. Nor is there, for the moment at least, either theological teaching or hierarchical orders specifying them.

It is the missionary experience of the primitive Church, reported in the scriptures at the time of the apostles, that permits us to extract what we can consider to be elements in every missionary act. Obviously, the missionary experience of the apostolic era was a privileged one. It was the direct outcropping of the mission of those men chosen by Christ to be his apostles. The word "apostle" is the key word. It contains all the missionary teaching collected by the apostolic tradition.

43

The word "apostle," from the Greek *apostolos,* means "one sent forth." This word belongs exclusively to the Christian language. Its equivalent in secular language is "mission." [1]

The apostle is sent to speak officially; he is the *messenger* of the Good News. The Word of God is entrusted to him so that he might proclaim it. "Go into the whole world and preach the Gospel to every creature" (Mk. 16, 15).

The apostle is the Word-carrier, the herald (from the Greek *kerux*). St. Paul, in the epistle to Timothy (2 Tim. 1, 11), directly associates the word "apostle" to that of "herald." From the word *kerux* is derived "kerygma," which means "declaration of the Word." The apostle was created to proclaim the Word; he must speak (Acts 4, 20).

What the apostle says is not said of himself (2 Tim. 1, 13). He comes as ambassador: "On behalf of Christ, therefore, we are acting as ambassadors, God, as it were, appealing through us" (2 Cor. 5, 20).

The apostle is an *ambassador*—that is, he acts as mediator between the one who sent him (1 Cor. 9, 1-3) and the one to whom he is sent. He must ask a question and elicit a response. What is that question if not one of faith? What is the answer if not conversion?

The apostle appears as one who arouses faith by provoking the response expressed by conversion (Acts 3, 12-19). Like every ambassador who shows his credentials, the apostle accredits the Word which he announces through signs (Mk. 16, 17). Essentially, the apostle is a *witness:* a witness of the resurrection; a witness of what he has seen and heard; a witness of Christ who lives in the community of which he is a member (Acts 1, 8; 4, 20; 1 Cor. 1, 5; 9, 7).

---

[1] It should be noted that the word "mission" comes from the Latin *mittere,* having exactly the same meaning as the Greek word *apostellein,* to send. It was only in the Middle Ages that it first appeared in the language of the Church. The theology of the epoch adapted the word to signify the gift of the three divine Persons to men. During the Renaissance, the term "missionary" appeared, referring to the apostles sent to evangelize far-off countries. In the 18th century, the Roman Congregation of Propaganda Fide consecrated this use of the term, employing the word "mission" exclusively in the sense of outside mission to foreign countries. During the same period, St. Vincent de Paul used the word to designate the interior missions re-Christianizing France.

| Messenger | Ambassador | Witness |
| of the Word | of the Faith | of the Church |

These are the three essential characteristics of all those who have been baptized and confirmed. They are the three characteristics of the entire missionary Church, the seeds of which were found in ancient Israel. Israel was sent to the neighboring people by God as an ambassador, with the character of messenger (Is. 40, 19), to be his witness to the nations (Is. 14, 10-12; 64, 8).

Word and Declaration
Faith and Conversion
Witness and Community

these are the three pairs which form the six parts of the missionary act. They must be found in every action which calls itself "missionary." These six elements form an interpretive grid, permitting the verification of the missionary value of each action. Whatever forms of action I take, whether I am active or not, militant or not, if I want my missionary action to meet these criteria, I ask myself these questions:

(a) How am I the messenger of the Good News?

(b) How am I the questioner who arouses faith by calling to conversion?

(c) How am I the witness-revealer of Christ risen in the Church?

Suppose, for example, that we choose the first of these pairs: Word-declaration. First, we must be aware of the primal importance of God's Word in missionary action. Scripture is the postulate of our faith, which is based essentially on revelation. If we can agree to the truth of God and cling to his person, it is because he makes himself known to us through his Word. We must know this Word if we hope to spread the knowledge of God and bring about the meeting of the unbeliever with the person of God. The Word is the very content of the mission; it powerfully carries the announcement of Jesus Christ.

The Word of God is *incisive;* it is *the* News—not just any news, but the Good News which concerns every person. The Word of God builds upon every person; it calls upon every person.

The Word of God is *decisive;* it concerns every person and engages every person to respond. It demands that we take part; it forces us to take a position; it judges us.

We are led to make the alarming acknowledgment that Christ is there, acting in his Word. He has put the Word at our disposal. Now we must discover how to announce that Word.

2. Proclamation of the Word in Missionary Action

How to Understand That Declaration

First of all, we must eliminate forgeries. There is no question of peddling the Word as sects do, no need to have the words of the Gospel always on our lips. The Word of God is proclaimed in the Church. The privileged place of the Word is the Christian community. The moment *par excellence* of the Word is the liturgical action. The Word is not besmirched any more than is the eucharist. It is sacred. It is not to be prostituted in any place or in any way. The exigencies of the catechumenate show us what preparation is necessary to keep from throwing the pearl to the swine. What, then, must we do?

First of all, we must strain our efforts to promote the climate and create the occasion where, in true dialogue, it will be possible to lead the unbeliever himself to want to question the Word. The declaration of the Word does not consist of reading, speaking, quoting and commenting on the Gospel. However, it does entail:

(a) Whetting the appetite of those who do not nourish themselves with the Word. You can always say to an unbeliever: "Listen, you ask me philosophical questions concerning the existence of God. You are impressed by the objections you raise. But just exactly what have you done up to now to get information? Have you ever tried going for these answers you seek to their very source, the Word of God? I am willing to discuss the matter with you, but first you must be willing to support your questions in terms of the answers you can find."

(b) Developing the transcendent character of the Word of God by the quality of our human words, which themselves give way that the Word might pass. Our human words serve as a translation of the Word of God. It is important that our words be faithful to the Word. If they are not, they obscure the Word. The Word must not be degraded by the merely human wisdom of our purposes. It is exactly for this reason that St. Paul reminds us: "What is wisdom in the eyes of men is foolishness in the eyes of God." That is why we must be sufficiently evangelized ourselves in order to communicate the contents of the Gospel without spoiling them by our sermonizing.

(c) Finally, and most essentially, placing the unbeliever in the presence of the Gospel. To evangelize, in the strict sense, does not mean to enter upon the apostolate, but to cause a meeting with the living Word. The unbeliever must be able to see in the life of the believer the symbols which he will rediscover when he is ready to read the Gospel for himself. This preview corresponds to the Old Testament, which allowed the Jews to greet the Word in their days. The *sine qua non* of this creation of "presence" is the Christian's respect for the life of the Word of God. Because it is living, it is progressive. We can rightly speak of the growth of the Word. In the Gospel, it is compared to a seed. The parable of the mustard seed illustrates the growth of the kingdom and can be applied to the Word of God.

In the Acts of the Apostles (6, 7) we are told with what attention the apostles, after Pentecost, observed the progress of the Word: "The Word of the Lord continued to spread." The Word does not escape the crises of growth in life. Too often we forget this and seem to think that, instantly and eternally, it can bear fruit and that one single isolated word of the Gospel could be decisive.

Therefore, the missionary should respect all these laws of life, and be patient, vigilant and persevering. He must develop the Word of God in hearts, give firmness to its area of growth, not telescope its moments of development, and be aware of the psychological and spiritual age of those who welcome it. All this is needed to prevent a growth-crisis which could harden into one fatal rejection.

An excessive concern in seeking a language accessible to the unbeliever is liable to result in detours instead of the preaching of the Gospel. Past generations were not so careful to prepare the terrain and respect the growing conditions of the Gospel. They twisted the Gospel so much that they ended in passing it by. The Gospel was watered with pious attentions; it was embroidered upon; it was copied. The Gospel "stories" were told so beautifully and so well that the true sense of the grace-provoking declaration was lost.

With all these conditions of presentation in mind, we must again find the strength of the declaration itself and know at certain moments—moments of grace—how to launch the Word. Wasn't that Christ's way? Didn't he say, purely and simply, what he had to say, at the risk of being taken for a fool?

The Contents of the Declaration

In a broad sense, it may be said that the New Testament presents the Christian message in the form of catechesis. The events of salvation are revealed with the intent to teach. They are reported in order to teach us what salvation is. This didactic framework is likely to hinder the unbeliever's access to the Gospel; that is one reason why it should not be quoted in just any old way. There is always the danger of attracting the unbeliever's attention more to the framework itself than to its contents.

The apostles did not proclaim the Gospel under the form in which we know it (they did not quote the Gospel because it had not yet been written). We must do as they did. They presented it totally and schematically, in an abridgment which might appear naive. They kept strictly to the essential: "There is no salvation except in Jesus Christ, dead and risen, who carries us with him."

This primitive declaration is called "kerygma." The literary style of kerygma is often close to exhortation. Primarily, it is a question aimed at proclaiming the Good News by opening hearts to conversion. The kerygma was spoken through inspiration and was not put into writing. However, traces of it can be found in the Acts of the Apostles, permitting us to reconstruct the outline of themes essential to the mission.

Obviously, we cannot pretend to announce the message today without going to the source of those who announced it in its purity. We have to extract the contents of these essential themes in order to determine which present-day values are capable of conveying these contents.

The kerygma [2] is presented according to a four-part plan:

[2] The kerygma is found principally in Acts 2, 14, 40; 3, 12-26; 4, 8-12, etc.

—*declaration of the event* of salvation in the person of Jesus, dead and risen;

—*significance of the event:* the kingdom is here; this is the moment of salvation;

—*significance of the person:* Christ is the Lord, the Son of God; salvation is he who performs it;

—all men are called to salvation: it is *conversion.*

We will limit ourselves to two aspects:

—how to announce Jesus Christ, dead and risen;

—how to announce salvation.

(a) *How to Announce Jesus Christ, Dead and Risen.* The historical fact of the resurrection must be bypassed in order to grasp its intense interior reality. The resurrection is the explosion of God's love, stronger than death; it is victory over sin. This is the content of the declaration. Men must be led to recognize in their lives the love they are capable of. We must teach them, beginning with very simple themes, that they are capable of love. To unveil to them the power of love which they can realize in themselves is to lead them to discover the risen Christ. How do we go about this?

By means of an event such as the death of someone dear, we must show them the power of love which was at the heart of the dead person's life and which no one recognized. This leads them to discover that, in their own lives, they had not been aware of that same power of love which is none other than Jesus Christ risen. This is the pre-announcement of the resurrection.

But, above all, it is in drawing the attention of the unbeliever to all the *positive* things there can be in his life and in those of his brothers that the announcement of the risen Christ is initiated. I should like, in this regard, to tell you about the witness of a priest, a personal witness and therefore inimitable. It was a curate from Nanterre who told me this: "The people I meet in the big new apartment developments live under the signs of sadness and boredom. Even things that might bring them well-being and comfort are underrated and judged negatively. The other day, I heard two women criticize the well-planned day nursery of a big development. I thought to myself: 'How can I preach the resurrection to these people who no longer want anything because they are disappointed by everything they once wanted?' I don't know how I went about it. First of all, I was opposed to this spirit of systematic criticism. Then I made them see, beyond all there might be to criticize, what good there was. For example, I emphasized the chance they had in comparison with that of preceding generations who never knew all the things we have today. I helped them to admire."

We can forget the incident, but let us retain what it indicates—namely, that capacity for admiration in the midst of mediocrity. Isn't it hope? And that capacity of opening to hope—isn't that the grace of the resurrection? To educate people by making them sensitive to the human values which underlie Christian values is to put them on the very path of the resurrection.

If there are objections to the distance which separates the mystery of the risen Christ and these feeble detours of the teaching of the faith, we must say that this distance is the terrain which must be prepared and surveyed so that the Holy Spirit might work. Our announcement very often consists only in preparing the ground for the work of the Holy Spirit.

This preparation of the terrain is the "human education" spoken of by Paul VI in his Encyclical *Ecclesiam suam:* "Our mission is the announcement of unquestionable truth and necessary salvation. It will not be presented armed with exterior coercion, but by the legitimate means of *human education,* interior persuasion, ordinary conversation." Ordinary conversation is that of the curate on the street, of a housewife on the steps, or of you yourself with a guest who unbends over coffee.

(b) *How to announce salvation.* It is difficult to put the unbeliever, already satiated in his self-complacency or indifferent in his skepticism, into a state of desiring salvation. What does salvation mean to him?

We must at least make him understand that for the Christian salvation is:

—not the arrival *on the shores of eternity* of a little soul lucky enough to escape the torments of hell because it was well preserved from the dangers of the earth as well as deprived of the pleasures of the earth;

—not, as esoteric religions are fond of saying, the guarantee of *individually* escaping sickness, unhappiness, anxiety and death, or the assurance of happiness;

—the happiness announced by the kerygma which is the participation in the alliance of God with men; it is the joy of participating in the achievement of creation in the fullness of time.

The essence of salvation is the community. It follows, then, that the human values most likely to bring about the discovery of the ecclesial dimension of salvation are values fitted to the world's dimensions. We mean, of course, the historical sense, to which we will return with regard to the dialogue between Christians and Marxists.

The historical sense which torments the contemporary mentality contains in great measure all the qualities of the alliance. The man who does not have that sense, at least vaguely, is not ready to welcome God's salvation. Thus, it is important to educate this sense of history because it helps to make the sense of salvation grow. To have the historical sense in everyday life means: [3]

—emerging from the sphere of personal interests, of individual human success;

—to recognize that what is important is the meaning of the entire world, and to give a meaning to the total human adventure;

—to become aware of the significance of all this, of the positive sense of freedom as compared to the physical and moral alienations which prevent easy entry upon a perspective of life and the world.

To discover all this is to unveil the contents of salvation announced by the kerygma: God comes in history to give it an absolute meaning.

Conclusion

It has been necessary to examine generalities because they shed light on the basic problems of the mission. But we cannot remain at this level. We must now make a practical resolution: to have the courage always to look at our missionary action in the light of the six elements comprising the missionary act.

Is our mission evangelization? What are the forms of action in which we are engaged? How do we put into our words the contents of the Word and the power of the declaration?

[3] We cite here the mimeographed notes Polycopiée from a course given by Fr. Liégé at the Catholic Institute of Paris: "II Special Pastoral Theology."

5 THE MISSIONARY ACT
Faith and Witness

The prize of the mission is faith: "More than ever, everything should hang on faith. If the mission is a success, it is faith which makes it so." [1] But what are the ways most likely to make faith grow? What ways are appropriate to the elements of the act of faith? What are the means required to allow the unbeliever to discover how to enter into this movement of faith which will cause him to meet God and cling to him?

It should be made clear that by an "act of faith" we do not mean that act which consists in affirming the revealed truths in which we believe, but rather the dynamism which puts into action the movement of adhesion of the man who binds himself to God. The act of faith is the interplay of grace and liberty which intervene, each with its own characteristics, in the movement of assent to God. The search for the signs appropriate to the act of faith permits the unbeliever to discover that they are not arbitrary but are the very expression of the mystery of God.

If the unbeliever had a better knowledge of the movement of the act of faith and to what it corresponds, he would assent to faith more easily. What is the process? What better way of discovering it than through that group of signs which make up Christian witness? The witness made by Christians should emphasize the very qualities of the act of faith likely to make the unbeliever see the step of faith as itself revealing the mystery of God.

We must forget the abstract definitions of faith and set out in the existential step of one who wants to adhere to God, who says either "I have faith" or "I do not have faith." When he says, "I have faith," what does he mean if not that faith is a movement of being which orients us toward God, which orders us to God? "I have faith" means, first of all: "I know that God is not a stranger

[1] Plenary Assembly of the French Episcopate, 1964.

53

in my life, that he is in my life." We can say, then, that *to believe in God is to be in touch with God.*

Have you considered that this relational characteristic of faith, which establishes this dependent relationship of man upon God, does not differ from the relationship which unites man to God in creation. In creating us, God calls us to live with him, to participate in his life. In doing this, God binds himself to us and us to him; here is all the mystery of the alliance which we make ours in faith. Faith is the recognition of that alliance, accepted and wanted as such. Faith incorporates all the characteristics of the alliance; it is expressed by a movement of call and response—the call of God and the response of man. To understand the mechanism of the act of faith, it should be considered simultaneously from God's side and from man's, a free and reciprocal engagement.

Characteristics of the Call

That call is a *universal grace.* All men are created by love. All men, without exception, are called to know God, to make an alliance with him, to live in the faith. "God our savior wishes all men to be saved" (1 Tim. 2, 4). Salvation is universal. The expression, "There is no salvation outside the Church," should be understood in this sense: Since it is the Church which makes real the universal call of God, the Church is the one to communicate salvation. If all men do not yet know God, it is not because God does not call them, but rather because the Church has not fully accomplished her mission.

The call is *a gift.* It is through pure love that God takes the initiative in calling all men to live with him and bestows upon them the gift of faith. God extends his sovereign liberty to man in leaving him free to accept or to refuse this gift. Thus the response of men has the same characteristic as God's call. It is essentially free.

Characteristics of Man's Response

This double movement of call and response results in the meeting of these two liberties: the total liberty of God who calls, and the total liberty of the man who answers as he wishes. The conditions of the life of faith reveal that fundamental liberty. God does not wish to impose himself upon men. For that reason, he presents himself as something we are looking for. If we can neither see nor touch God, how can we desire him?

Man's Response Is Pure Liberty

Man's response is pure liberty, because God has no more need for man than man has for God. That God has no need of man is a fact as obvious to the believer as to the unbeliever. If the unbeliever accepts the hypothesis that God exists, he admits at the same time that God is sovereign master. To say that "God needs men" is one way of making understood God's free will to include all men in his plan of salvation by calling them to be the artisans of their own destinies. This participation of man in his own salvation obscures in no way the mystery of God as transcendent being. It is still obvious that God would deny himself if he were in a dependent state.

To pretend that man has no need of God is the whole question of Marxism, a problem of faith. To the Christian, this pretension appears blasphemous: Isn't man essentially a contingent creature and therefore dependent upon his creator?

There is reason to make a fundamental distinction between the metaphysical level, where man defines himself in relation to God, and the psychological level, where man defines himself in relation to himself. On the ontological level, it is obvious that man can do nothing without God. Man's frailty brings out the evidence of his need of God. On the existential level, man's independence is total. He can do without God—that is to say, man psychologically does not need to know how he belongs to God and to recognize it as such in order to "live his life." He has no need of attributing to God the marvels of creation in order to admire the beauty of nature. He does not even need charity to love men, his brothers. That is the witness of the Marxist *praxis;* it is the message of the generous atheism represented by Camus, for example.

With this distinction in mind, it is possible to say: "If man needs God in order to be, he does not need him in order to exist."

This gap between the ontological and existential levels permits us to better understand the sense in which we pretend that man has no need of God. The liberty of men in adhering to faith does not rest on the need of God but on the possibility of recognizing God as his creator. Because God does not force men to answer his call, the response of faith is pure liberty. Man's response belongs entirely to him. It is a choice of his intelligence which may know God, of the will which gives God its adherence, and of the sensibility which gives its consent to him.

Man's Answer Is a Choice

At the level of *intelligence,* the mysteries of faith do not force themselves upon reason. To be sure, the proofs of God's existence are not to be scoffed at. They carry a light which permits us to locate the mystery, but they cannot pretend to penetrate it. Faith will never be the result of philosophical proofs. For that reason, it is useless to argue with the unbeliever. Faith will never come in terms of demonstration. One enters into the movement of faith with this seemingly paradoxical conviction: the point of departure of faith does not rest on a *priori* evidence of God's existence, but on the certitude that, since he does exist, he will be found.

On the level of intellectual logic, we have to admit that to believe in something, we must be sure it exists. We cannot believe in a phantom. Faith's knowledge is different: God is known as a living person. What is important in my knowledge is not that a certain person exists in himself, but that he exists for me. First, we must have the personal experience of God as he reveals himself in order to be able to reassure ourselves of his existence.

Faith is essentially a way of knowledge through love (philosophers say by connaturality). This method of knowledge implies a bypassing of rational categories to grasp something reason cannot accept at the conceptual level. It does not demand resignation of spirit, but a real humility which consists of accepting the limitations of intelligence in order to exceed them and recognize what Pascal said: "Reason's supreme step is to recognize that there are an infinite number of things which surpass it. True Christianity consists of the submission and use of reason."

The method of faith's knowledge supposes a triple step:

(a) an *inductive* step: that of the seeker who arrives at his conclusion after believing in his hypothesis;

(b) an *existential* step: that of Pascal, for example, as summed up in his famous: "You would not seek me if you had not found me." Faith's knowledge is totalizing: it involves the whole being, not only the intelligence, but will and sensibility. We go to God with all our strength; he cannot be grasped as a purely intellectual object. Faith is not adherence to a doctrine of logical proofs, but to a person;

(c) a step of *love,* that of revelation. The Lord never starts by proving that he is God. It is enough for him to make a sign, to speak with authority. He demanded that Abraham consent to the call addressed to him: "Leave everything." And it was thus, by involving his whole life at the simple Word of the Lord, that Abraham discovered who God is. He discovered who God is before knowing that God is.

At the level of *will,* of intellectual *adherence,* the attachment to God in the person of Christ is upheld by the will. It is this which permits the spirit to consent to things it does not understand.

At the *behavioral* level of action, this attachment to the person of Christ presumes a life of relation with God which equally involves the will. To be attached to God means to orient the whole being to live in conformity to Christ's life. To act out faith is to do the will of God, to live the Gospel. But because it is impossible to live the Gospel without being animated by love, the involvement of the will requires the engagement of all the affective forces of the person.

At the level of *sensibility,* just as the intelligence must exceed its limits to attain God, so must one's sensibility exceed itself. A great deal of emotional detachment is necessary. God, in the realm of intelligence, demands a quality of spirit capable of giving up intellectual satisfaction. Likewise, in the realm of sensibility, he demands a quality of heart capable of giving up emotional consolation.

To have faith is not to be aware of God. It is to consent to being possessed by him in order to possess him. The adherence to God is consent.

This interplay of grace and the constitutional liberty of the act of faith brings out the fact that to accept the rules of a life of faith is to live an adventure. Faith is often presented as a risk to run, a bet to make. This notion of risk and bet is bound up with the concept of arbitration. There is nothing hazardous in faith. It is better to say that faith is an adventure, because adventure always includes one uncertain element which demands courage and a spirit of enterprise, and one certain part which permits us to engage ourselves with confidence.

WITNESS AND COMMUNITY

Characteristics of Witness

Witness is the expression of the evangelistic necessity to be the light of the world. St. Paul summed up this exigency in very simple terms: "For we take forethought for what is honorable not only before God but also in the sight of men" (2 Cor. 8, 21). This need of radiance, however, should not lead us to confuse witness with good example. The idea of good example is colored by a moralism which risks rapid degeneration into an attitude of superiority and insupportable pharisaism. The Christian is not a professor of virtue who demonstrates the benefits and merits of his qualities. Witness is in no way a question of giving a lesson or a moral. It is not to gain the satisfaction of being found impeccable that the Christian concerns himself with setting a good example for the unbeliever. Rather, it is to avoid giving the unbeliever reasons for justifying himself.

Just as he does not try to impose his morality, neither does the Christian attempt to indoctrinate by the strength of his ideas. Understood or rejected, he knows that the aim of witness is not to convince or prove but to open to the unbeliever the possibility of engaging his liberty with regard to God. Consequently, it is not a question of wanting to conquer at any price. Only the truth and unselfishness of the witness can be the persuasive forces.

Witness is a form of dialogue in which the persons encountering each other become capable of appreciating one another. It is a silent dialogue implying respect for the other person and detachment from everything which would attach importance to oneself. Humility is the criterion of true witness. Often we are unaware that we are bearing witness.

But there is no dialogue without confrontation. That is why bearing witness will many times mean taking a position. The Christian is essentially someone who reveals. To be "the salt of the earth" sometimes means to produce that salt! It happens fairly often that a Christian finds himself inextricably involved in situations, trapped by his actions into being an accomplice of things he condemns in theory.

If he can't change the course of events, it is still the Christian's duty to protest. He should admit his own inability to do what he says. He should never justify in principle what he is forced to do, defectively, in action. For example, just because certain soldiers were forced to torture during the war in Algeria does not mean that torture is justifiable. Péguy said, in a violent way: "Who does not speak the truth, though he knows he thus makes himself accomplice of liars and counterfeiters?" It is through the choices which engage the life of a Christian that his witness reveals the life of Christ.

If the Christian gives witness by squarely taking a position, he reveals equally in showing what the love of God is. As Christ revealed the love of his Father to men, so the Christian reveals that love by the charity in which he lives. To bear witness is to permit the unbeliever to discern the imprint of the Trinity in the life of the witness. To bear witness is to become visibly what, since baptism, we have been invisibly—members of the body of Christ in such a way that the unbeliever may say of the Christian: "It is no longer he who lives, but Christ who lives in him."

Finally, to bear witness is to reveal that Christ is a living person. If we do not show this, we cannot pretend to call unbelievers to the faith, because faith involves one's entire life. Only a living person is capable of involving his whole life. It is in giving his life an evangelical quality that the Christian becomes, to the unbeliever, a question to which only God can be the answer. He bears witness to the extent that, by creating mystery, he inspires the desire to believe in Jesus Christ. It remains then to reveal Jesus Christ as a living person.

To reveal Christ as someone, the witness must underline his person-to-person relationship. Christian witness should also contain the specifically evangelical values which Christ especially loved; these values are the signs of the free and universal love of God and are alone capable of justifying Christian fidelity. The witness should bring out the fact that these values are the same as those of the alliance—pardon, mercy, poverty, joy: basic values of the act of faith which are rediscovered and transposed into gratuity, catholicity, liberty and trust.

Since the structure of the act of faith takes on the mysterious characteristics of the alliance, Christian witness should bear these values of the alliance in such a way that the unbeliever may discover, through the very structure of the act of faith, the revelation of God's love in his alliance. We should note that these values in the alliance are precisely those which most correspond to the unbelieving world's expectations.

Contents of Christian Witness

Among the values of the Gospel which should be an integral part of witness are those which we have already mentioned: pardon, poverty, joy and mercy.

Pardon is not a decrease of guilt but an increase of love. Whoever pardons gives beyond the requirements of strict justice. Because it demands of a Christian that he rise beyond what is normally and legitimately due and pass to the free level of love, pardon is a living sign revealing that free call of God which takes note neither of faults nor of merits, but only of love.

Poverty is the evidence of the love of a man who can detach himself from perishable things in order to attach himself to the essential—that is, God. Poverty expresses the fundamental attitude of confidence which is at the heart of the act of faith and the mystery of the alliance.

Joy is the full expression of the beatitudes. It is the assurance that God can perfectly crown the life of the man who, having perfectly believed in God, finds happiness in him. It is the sign of success in a life lived in the liberty of having chosen God.

Mercy is salvation spread out and communicated. It is the love with which God saves us.

Zacchaeus, Mary Magdalene, the adultress of whom St. John speaks, the prostitute whom the Gospel says will precede us in the kingdom of heaven, and the words and parables of the Lord all point to this conclusion: "There is more joy over one sinner who repents than over a hundred just who have no need of repentance." The whole Gospel reveals Christ's great love for sinners. The faces of these sinners are unknown to us. They seem very distant, without substance, reduced to the clichés of sermons. We cannot visualize those to whom Jesus spoke. We think of them as "some poor souls" or "some faceless people."

Yet we find these sinners in our everyday lives. Who can look at them with love? To be sure, entertainers can make sympathetic characters of drunks and prostitutes for our amusement. But, seriously, who other than the Christian can look at them with love? The Christian has exclusive rights to this witness of love because Christ was the only one who could truly love sinners.

Look at Christ; his attitude is very simple. First of all, he believes in the love of his Father for all those who are lost in the sight of the world. He believes that, despite the sin which disfigures them, this love endows them with the dignity of God's children. He does not despair; he loves them as they are. He neither exonerates nor rejects them for their guilt. He knows they are responsible, but he does not use this as an excuse to condemn them. He knows they are sinners; that is why he saves them.

To the extent that the Christian makes Christ's attitude his own, he bears witness to the folly of welcoming those whom the world judges to be lost. This witness would be difficult for the Christian to give individually. If it is not lived in a community, on a collective level, he is likely to dissipate his strength ineffectively. The witness of mercy must be borne by the community in order to reveal the universal love of God as communicated by the family of the Church.

Take, for example, the witness which our community at Saint-Severin tried, with difficulty and some doubt, in the reception of the hobos, beatniks and poor aliens among us. This welcome was essentially missionary in character, a witness of mercy to those who have no community.

Isn't such a witness likely to make the real residents of the neighborhood discover that a Christian community does not rely on worldly wisdom for such a welcome, but rather on the foolishness of God's love? The unbeliever—and how many "believers" are not just that in this respect?—who thinks in terms of earthly laws is forced to question himself when faced with what he considers to be the clumsiness of Christians who busy themselves with the ungrateful poor, the dangerous drifters, the parasites.

Isn't this too often our attitude? What do we hear? "These are not worthy people. They are vice-ridden. They give a bad example

to our children. They are dying from laziness and alcoholism."
What's more, it's true! All these are people whom we call "public
sinners"; they do not hide the face of their sin as "nice" people do,
and so they are judged by society.

We can agree that the world's judgment is correct. But it is
precisely because this is the case that Christ's love can penetrate
where it is needed, by means of the Christian's solicitude. Christ
came to save whoever is lost. It is to the extent that the Christian
overcomes his selfishness and the world's wisdom to make this
senseless salvation his own that he bears witness to the universal
love of Christ calling all men to faith.

Bearing witness begins where the world's wisdom stops. The
Christian, who sees as clearly as the world and who acts with
knowledge of his cause, goes beyond the justness of worldly reasons to the light of God's reason.

To bear witness is to manifest the logic of God. How can we
expect unbelievers to embrace Christ the savior when Christians,
witnesses of salvation, make judgments that contradict salvation
and neutralize it? To be sure, a very real courage is necessary to
rid oneself of the prejudices of public opinion. We are paralyzed in
inertia. We are afraid of being inconvenienced by the ultimate
consequences of salvation. We prefer to live as if salvation did not
exist, as if mercy belonged only to the legend of God.

However, this love of mercy which befits a Christian may reveal
the very nature of God's love. To bear witness in this world, which
refuses the madness of love, often means protesting this pharisaical
mentality, proclaiming the love of mercy whatever the odds.

Welcomed or misunderstood, the Christian is convinced that to
bear witness is to consent to transmit the signs of salvation without
the expectation of any effectiveness other than that of knowing
that he has become a stumbling block. The value of witness is not
judged by its results. That is why it would be out of place to ask
those who bear witness for their campaign balance sheet.

If the witness is successful, it will end in faith. And if faith
emerges, it will find strength in itself and produce the mission.

II

LISTENING TO THE WORLD
Missionary Action

6 MEETING THE UNBELIEVER

I

THE MEETING POINT

The man of the 20th century, fiercely jealous of his dual liberty of opinion and expression, sets tolerance at the top of the values of our times. Although set so high, it is nevertheless not lacking in ambiguity. It embraces the qualities required for dialogue: broadmindedness, openness, respect for people, receptiveness to every idea, universal interest. Motivated by the generosity which characterizes it, tolerance has a natural inclination to elasticity. "Understanding" is easily transformed into laxity, broadmindedness into eclecticism. Thus, it is convenient to say, for example: "All religions have value."

Tolerance must learn to unite flexibility and firmness. Tolerance becomes intolerable if it gives up on the essentials, if it abandons the truth it should reveal. It is no longer tolerant if it fixes on minor things. That is the tendency of the "integrists" who think that religion is changed because forms evolve. On the other side are those who are carried away by progress and who, in the name of development, want to change the intangible character of fixed values.

Tolerance is found at the crossroads where believers and unbelievers meet. The believer, whose faith has been purified and deepened by evidence, is ready to walk the tightrope of dialogue with perfect balance. Worry about rejoining the unbeliever will not upset him. The flexibility which demands consideration of contrary opinions will not make him give way. The obvious contradictions in the unbeliever will not make him stumble. Thus, solidly established in faith, the believer is ready to take seriously the difficulties which create obstacles for the unbeliever.

He is not surprised to find among those close to him an almost total indifference and an absence of all religious concern. He is not the dupe of the intellectual coquetry of sophisticated agnostics who delight in dissertations on religious problems. He is not impressed by the vulgarity of critics or the adolescence of intellectual bullies. Nevertheless, he remains open to everyone, welcoming every idea, attentive to the smallest gesture, receptive to the tiniest crumb of truth.

He knows that, through this awkwardness of expressing the confused and inexact beliefs he alleges, the unbeliever is trying to say something which he has difficulty in communicating. He accepts the fact that the unbeliever may not know why he cannot believe. He does not attribute to laziness, nor even to ill will, the inability of the unbeliever to open himself to faith. The first form of tolerance is the respect which the believer shows for the unbeliever.

That believer whose faith imposes itself with the force of absolute evidence and is expressed without having been sufficiently purified and reflected upon risks judging shortsightedly the multitude of those who cannot believe. Minimizing the difficulties of the unbeliever, he reduces them to evasion: "Doesn't the unbeliever blind himself? Through pride or inability to conform his life to faith, doesn't he justify the reasons which he gives himself for not believing?"

This tendency to beg the question reveals the weakness of the believer who is incapable of admitting the phenomenon of unbelief. Disarmed by this unyielding fact, he looks for consoling explanations or second-rate solutions. This was the attitude of a certain apologetic idealist who could only imagine the problem of unbelief in metaphysical terms. He felt that as long as man is ontologically oriented toward God, it is not crucial that he can in fact do without him psychologically. To be sure, men's lack of satisfaction in their search for happiness can be interpreted as failure in the quest for God, but we do not have the right to make hasty decisions.

At the philosophical level, it is easy to agree that the aspirations of men are the expression of an implicit desire for God and, finally, the sign of faith in the making. At the existential level, this thirst for the absolute—the sign of a certain search—is not identical with the thirst for God. Between the two there is still a wide breach. We do not have the right to say that "an unbeliever is a believer who doesn't know it." How many times have we heard this: "Why not take the unbeliever as he is, making use of his feelings?" It is not rare to see a Christian defending some author with the excuse that his inspiration is in harmony with the message of Christ. If someone wishes to declare himself an unbeliever, let us recognize his right to assert himself as such!

The second form of tolerance is the elementary honesty which recognizes the right of the unbeliever to exist as such, even when in our eyes he conducts himself like a Christian. The more awkward we are at grasping the phenomenon of unbelief, the more we should admit our humility and inadequacy. We should have the courage to admit our limitations in face of the resistance of unbelief. We must give up that pretense of always having an answer to everything, that ease which might give the impression that the Christian, unable to resolve the problems posed by faith, embraces mysteries without difficulty. Only the attitude of humility can help us to resist the temptation to triumphantly display a faith which will insult anyone who does not believe in it. The unbeliever does not want the believer to give good reasons for believing: more often, he wants him to know when to be quiet. Silence is the third form of tolerance.

II

MEETING THE UNBELIEVER

1. The Thinkers

(a) *The Militant Atheist.* In the mass of those who do not believe, the militant atheist represents a certain elite. Being generous, he gives meaning to his life. Capable of sacrifice, he does not weigh his difficulties in attaining the ideal he so relentlessly pursues. His atheism involves his life; it is a humanism. Because he believes in man, because he puts his hope in the world, the militant atheist belongs to the race of believers. Depending on the case, he believes despite God or without God. At any rate, he is a believer in a cause. His atheism is a faith.

The faith of the militant atheist rests in his concern to orient and accelerate the world in the foreseeable direction of its development. His faith is the power which he has over the world. Thus, God is no problem for him. The problem is the world. He does not demand that his personal life have meaning. His life is the life of all men, and the life of all men has meaning—the meaning of history.

Only the man of action, vitally interested in the world, can truly get in touch with the militant atheist. For this type of unbeliever, the meaning of dialogue is action. It is not the ideas of the Christian which impede the unbeliever, but the incapacity, engendered by these ideas, to transform the world. For the unbeliever, only the Christian's power to transform the world can be the proof of God's action on the world. It seems, then, that even if it be only by the quality of his action, the believer can lead the unbeliever to discover the reality of the kingdom of God on earth.

The final purpose of the Christian's action should be clarified by the motives activating him. The unbeliever does not ask the Christian to justify his reasons for loving the world, for he is only interested in the results. Simple dialogue with unbelievers, especially with Marxists, quickly becomes ambiguous. It is therefore important to make it clear that the history which guides the Christian is the history of salvation as presented by the Gospel.

We must know how to develop the dynamism of action contained in the Gospel and expressed by Christ by recalling the necessity of application: "It is not those who say 'Lord, Lord,' who will enter into the kingdom of heaven, but those who put the Word of God into action." This Word of God throughout the Gospel is an incessant invitation to bear fruit, to fructify our talents. God reveals himself in the Trinity like an acting force: "My Father and I work without cease."

Thus, perhaps, by the witness of action, the unbeliever will be inclined to believe that the kingdom of God is not a stranger in the land of men. Christ said many times: "The kingdom of God is in the midst of you." This kingdom of God, which opens on eternity, is already near. It does not consist of the refusal of those who resign from the world, but is rather the meaning behind the work of those who believe in the reconstruction of the world. The kingdom of God is but the completion of the city of men on earth. It is not the refuge of those who ensure their eternity by leading a timid existence on earth; it is a conquest by those who renew, in the power of the Spirit, the face of the earth. Finally, we must be familiar with the unbeliever's mentality in order to know what approach might represent an evangelical affirmation. For him, revelation has significance only through the significance of the world.

(b) *The Intellectual Atheist.* The militant atheist refuses to become entangled in philosophical considerations. The intellectual, however, approaches faith as a problem, in terms of reason. Through concern for his personal destiny, he seeks a meaning to his life and wonders if faith is not the possible answer to his search. For him, the main difficulty was his belief that faith is incompatible with reason. Faced with a mystery which is beyond his comprehension—namely, that revelation which he must acknowledge, and the dogmas to which he must submit—the man of reason considers himself condemned to intellectual suicide.

It is revelation, commanding attention as *a priori* to all knowledge, which is so difficult for the unbeliever to accept. God can be known only by beginning with God. Revelation is presented in an absolute way as the key to a system, and it seems that man must receive it passively, without discussion. This leaves man no possibility of inventing God. God is imposed upon him. The man of reason feels frustrated in his freedom, bound in his search by this categorical imperative which appears contradictory to him. Logically, to receive the Word of God, one must first believe that God exists. In presenting the fact of revelation like a petition, this logic is reversed, since now it is revelation which must first be admitted to discover that God exists.

This petition seems more difficult for the unbeliever to accept than the notion of mystery. Mystery presents itself to him "like a mental fireball, unabsorbable, without organic tie to the assembly of human knowledge." [1] But revelation is imposed like an intolerable absolute which rapidly becomes the core of the inclination to disbelieve. It is easy to understand the distress of the unbeliever of goodwill when he comes upon this stumbling block in his search.

The only justification which the Christian can give for the *a priori* character of revelation is the sovereign authority of God who freely reveals himself as he wishes. Rather than base the absolute character of revelation upon the argument of authority, so difficult for the unbeliever to admit because it is indisputable, why not humbly admit to sharing the unbeliever's difficulty? We have no argument to advance, but an attitude to propose—that of confidence: "I put my hope in the Lord; I am sure of his Word." This loyal attitude places us once again, with regard to the unbeliever, in the only climate bearable for him: that of poverty. We do not

[1] P. Henry, *Parole et Mission.*

try to justify, but only invite the unbeliever to agree to have the experience of God: "Those who trust in the Lord will not be disappointed." Unless he is a resolute freethinker, even the satisfied unbeliever can only be respectful when confronted with this humble attitude of the believer.

It happens that certain unbelievers are deliberate freethinkers. The freethinker is one who, refusing the *a priori* character of Christian confidence, affects an air of superiority and indifference when confronted with what he considers to be the obscurantism of religion. He is fond of all that might be judged incompatible between faith and science. He does not fail to stir up big, impressive problems such as evil and the scandalous suffering of the innocent. He takes the occasion to put revelation, which he refuses, into contradiction with the facts which he supports—for example, if God loves humanity, why do men suffer?

What attitude should be adopted toward the unbeliever who steels himself in this way? Let us use Christ as our example. Didn't he come up against this sort of feeling from certain Pharisees and Sadducees? The Sadducees also fixed their refusal to accept Christ upon their refusal to believe in the resurrection.

Christ's attitude with disputers was always clear. He did not get lost in a maze of arguments. He always spoke the truth as it is. He led disputants to see the truth in the questions he asked. He helped them to discern the true and the false motivations behind their questions. Christ did not hesitate to discontinue the dialogue when it seemed impossible. After the multiplication of the loaves, didn't he slip away? That was not rejecting dialogue, but refusing to get lost in the impasses of false dialogue. The attitude of Christ can help us to locate ourselves with regard to the freethinker, to the extent that Christ came closer to the disputer who was the Pharisee.

But what was Christ's attitude toward the unbeliever whom we call the "intellectual atheist"? First of all, it should be pointed out that Christ was not confronted by atheists, for it was to a religious people that he announced the Good News. The enemies of Christ who refused his witness did not refuse it in the name of any atheism but in the name of their religion. They went even further; in the name of their law they killed their prophets and put their God to death. It was in the name of their faith that they acted like unbelievers before Christ.

We find this same attitude in the unbeliever of today. Living in a civilization of pseudo-Christianity, he is contaminated by the virus of religion in spite of himself. It is in the name of that religion that he refuses to believe, confusing the epiphenomena of religious fact with the essentials of faith. We find ourselves with regard to unbelievers in the same situation as Christ found himself with the Jews. The reception of the message of Christ by the Jews was hindered by the religious climate of that era. In these days, too, it seems that the superstructures of our Christian civilization veil the purity of the Gospel to unbelievers.

Though Christ did not confront the militants of unbelief, he was in contact with the pagans. As presented by the Gospel, the pagans were more open to Christ's message than the religious Jews. They welcomed the Word of God; they believed in it; they entered directly into contact with Christ. We recall the Roman officer at Capharnaum, the Syro-Phoenician and the Samaritan women.

Christ never failed to show his admiration for these unbelievers —at least those who, sociologically, were classed as such. By their disposition of heart and spirit, they were the true believers of the Gospel. It is true that they approached Christ for selfish reasons, but their desire to open up to him was evident. They showed signs of sympathy before asking him questions; they wanted to enter into the universe of him whom they discovered; they expressed their desire to believe.

Thus, when the experience of meeting Christ is begun without prejudice, intellectual questions solve themselves; not that they dissolve, but they no longer appear as insurmountable obstacles. They give way to the answer of life communicated by the Word of God in the faithful adherence to Christ.

2. The Non-Intellectuals

Theologians and theoreticians of atheism analyze the causes of unbelief as if the world were inhabited uniquely by intellectuals and the causes of unbelief were reducible to difficulties of an intellectual order. But the unbeliever whom we meet every day on the street is the man with no reason to believe or disbelieve, and this is precisely what troubles us.

The subtle analyses of contemporary atheism fall apart when applied to explain the unbelief of the man in the street. He doesn't believe because he doesn't have time or he doesn't want to, or he doesn't have the courage. He considers that it's too complicated; the Gospel is strange to him, a series of improbable affirmations.

What does it mean, to the man who takes his subway every morning, that Jesus was raised up three days after his death? What difference does it make that our God is God in three Persons? It is useless to say to this man that God loves humanity. What does that change for him? Does he see the effects of it? The man in the street approaches faith in a practical way, wanting to know what good is religion. How can we make him aware of something which appears so strange and so unnecessary?

When he expresses his objections, he does so in a manner so fragmentary that we are disconcerted. He speaks of a caricature. These objections are usually impassioned because they emerge from life: "I don't believe. . . . When I was a child, a priest slapped me"; "I don't believe. . . . My next-door neighbor, who was a good Christian, collaborated with the Nazis"; "I don't believe. . . . My boss, who calls himself a Christian, is unfair and exploits us"; "I don't believe. . . . The Church, who says she is for the poor, is fond of ostentation. Look at Rome!"

The griefs of the man in the street are cries from the heart, based upon diverse facts. General ideas are discussed—beginning with particular ones—in such a way that the dialogue gets bogged down in detail. Many unbelievers wave the flag of scandal, stirring up isolated cases which become the emblem of their refusal to believe—for example, the unfortunate attitude of a priest or Christian is used as an excuse.

But, on the other hand, the same people who recognize the positive witness of an individual Christian or priest restrain themselves from generalizing positively so as to accept faith. They say: "If everyone were like him, I would believe." But they stop right there. Why does everyone have "to be like him" for them to believe, when the counter-witness of one single Christian is enough to justify their refusal to believe? Touching illogic!

Must it be recalled that the art of dialogue consists of going beyond a contest of arguments *ad hominem?* And must we be reminded of the necessity of distinguishing questions of fact and of principle? That is what Christ shows us in his conversation with the Samaritan woman. The Samaritan interprets the transcendent message of the Lord through the everyday cares which assail her spirit. Christ invites her to see farther than her material preoccupations. He raises the level of the conversation in asking her the real questions which most profoundly touch her. If Christ in the Gospel seems to turn aside the questions asked him, it is essentially to make us understand that the question asked is not the real question intended.

Thus it appears that the art of missionary dialogue often consists not in giving the answer, but rather in restating the real question which the interlocutor did not know how to formulate. Missionary dialogue should be content to tentatively accept anything short of absolute rejection. It supposes an alert psychological sensitivity to people and a knowledge of the environment of the unbeliever. But what are the repercussions of his environment on the reactions of the unbeliever?

III
AMONG THE SIGNS OF OUR TIMES

The man of today already can foresee the appearance of the world of the future. The success of science fiction, the mania for continued progress, the complex of characteristics which inhibit us when it comes to simply defining our civilization—all these are indications of an epoch which is not its own master. According to the particular center of each one's interest, our civilization is, at the same time, that of the conquest of interplanetary space, nuclear weapons, nylon and plastic; it is that of telecommunication, automation and speed, and so on. With all this change, our civilization could scarcely escape the mishaps and paradoxes of all evolution. For the employed of the West, it is already a civilization of leisure, whereas for the underdeveloped nations, it is not yet even one of work. At one and the same time, it is a civilization which promotes the individual and collectivism. The entire world is turned upside down to find the serum which will save a baby from leukemia, while at the same time (not to mention the systematic massacres in extermination camps) people are killed by the millions and progress is made in the art of torture. Genius, progress, heroism, absurdity, savagery—all are combined under one sign.

What diagnosis can be made of our times? What repercussions

will the laws of this world have upon the mentality of contemporary man? How can the unbeliever be reached in this world of paradoxes which cannot even find itself? We have only a confused notion of the conditioning to which the presentation of the Good News is submitted. How can we locate and answer the eternal questions which are asked today in terms of the style and condition of our epoch? How can we find the elements of response to the problems of today? How can we find a common language, accessible to everyone, that will be valuable in making an overture to faith?

There is the whole question of discerning the signs of our times. To try to interpret these signs does not mean to pretend to find the solution to the problems they raise, but rather to look at the world in order to better grasp the conditions of the unbeliever. To be aware of the fabric of the present times is to ready ourselves for meeting the unbeliever. The first task is to learn how to look at the world. Beyond his personal reasons which create difficulties for him on the intellectual level, the unbeliever must be met at the crossroads of all life's currents, which make of his individual unbelief a collective fact.

1. Money

Mammon is not a new god of the world, but this god of the new world in which we live appears with the look of our times— that of speculation. Things are no longer judged on their inherent values but on what they bring or what they are worth in terms of particular situations. The economy being that of supply and demand, the law of commerce is that of the highest bid. Apartment buildings are not constructed to give dwellers a comfort worthy of human beings, but, before all else, to give the highest possible return in rent. It is not aesthetics which governs the laws of architecture, nor human factors which predominate; it is money.

Money is no longer a god adored for itself. It is worshiped for what it procures, though what it procures is incessantly depreciating. P. Henry says: "It is there that I place the malaise of collective man and the malaise of us all. Things are no longer means of exchange; the abundance of goods devaluates them. That is terrible, because the thing loses its value, like a sign of human relations. The gift is altered; charity becomes scandalous or impossible; poverty cannot be understood." [2]

2. Immediacy of Life

By this apparently curious word, we mean that sort of life lived from day to day, without enthusiasm or revolt. It is the daily existence confined within the close limits of banality. Man makes his hole in life. He digs his hole like Antigone dug her tomb, to be buried alive there. The more he wants to live, the more deeply does he plunge into the life which buries him. The causes of the burial of this life, shaded by the color of the times, are eternal— selfishness, mediocrity, faintheartedness, rich pleasure. But what is the sign of our times?

Instability and Insecurity

Our grandparents lived in an atmosphere of relative security which encouraged them to provide for tomorrow. To be sure, wars occurred, but they still had an accidental character of reparable catastrophe. They did not keep mothers from piling up in their closets reserves of sheets and dish towels for their marriageable daughters. The new worldly politics, with East and West opposed in two blocs, has changed the face of war. If war should break out in just one single spot on the earth, all the continents would tremble.

In addition to that law of war, all the factors of modern life have contributed to create this climate of uncertainty. Think, for example, of the almost constant menace represented by an automobile trip. Death is on the road, and we accommodate ourselves to it. A woman made this revealing admission: "I prefer to go 120 miles an hour in my sports car. I don't risk any more accidents than in a less powerful car, and, in case of an accident, I have an extra chance of being killed immediately!"

Since we don't know what the future holds in store, why complicate existence in the present moment? Since, on the other hand, we no longer have time to waste time, we have to make use of the present moment. It is the unpoetic civilization of the ready-to-

[2] P. Henry, in *Parole et Mission*.

wear, lost-and-found, self-service, nylon socks and paper napkins. Why mend, why iron, when we can just throw it away? Thus we separate the useful from the agreeable, but so what? The goal of a life of seeking is too far off, so we content ourselves with a flat and horizonless life which should be full but which eludes us.

Uniformity of Consumer Goods

"The growing reign of quantity carries in its wake the constant sameness of beings and things. Whether they are made in France or in the United States, products resemble each other: planes and cars, cameras, movies, radios and television sets." [3] Everywhere people tend to have access to the same consumer goods. This movement toward uniformity is translated by a conditioning of the masses where men no longer think.

3. Conditioning the Masses

Man, led by the fashions and molded by the multiple means of propaganda, has become the plaything of a generalized psychological trend.

The press, without foreseeing the repercussion of its news on "uninformed" people, daily throws at the anonymous but "tested" crowd its ration of the original and sensational. From psychoanalysis to birth control, all subjects are dragged through the mud. Everyone has read, under the hairdryer or in the subway, the latest bit of scandal. They talk about everything without knowing anything. It is the reign of pseudo-culture which encourages snobbishness and falsifies human relations.

Publicity plants dreams, illusions, phantasms. Exploiting men's gregarious instinct and collective mimicry, it has succeeded in creating the "average man." Viewed through the results of investigations and Gallup Polls which reduce him to pure ideas, man has become the image of the portrait given to him of himself. He is that distinguished man in the cigarette ads in all the magazines; he is the "ladies' man," thanks to this cologne or that shaving cream.

[3] P. Henry, *op. cit.*

Associating itself with the power of ambition, the desire to succeed, the thirst for prestige and the ambiguity of "sexualism" (as opposed to sexuality),[4] publicity has succeeded in making man surrender to conformity and sacrifice to idols.

Thus, like the man in the film, *Woman of the Dunes,* condemned to live literally engulfed in a pit, 20th-century man, swept along by the sands of existence, can no longer get his bearings. He is lost in his own mirages and led astray by the false prophets of the century. He is reduced personally to being only the inert mass which he reaffirms collectively in the world.

These external forces lessen man's power to react to the multiple surroundings which mold him. But the "class law," in a more cunning and diffuse way, suffocates him. This class law has a considerable hold on all men living in society and finding themselves always in small groups. This hold is still more considerable on young people, who are much more dependent upon the classes which they form: school, youth movements, etc. The present collective factors which condition the world of the young are well known: the phenomenon of "gangs," the frenzy for idols, vacation escapades, unending parties, etc.

All these factors reduce boys and girls to being no more than the group to which they belong. Educational movements, Christian or not, unwittingly are caught up in the current. Through laudable concern for opening to others, the young people's Catholic Action effects concern for one another. On the level of education in community living, this is very desirable, but sometimes it seems to be detrimental to a personal formation. If the young person is always considered in terms of the group, he is liable never to be awakened to the responsibility which he should have with regard to himself. The sense of personal effort and the taste for free culture are sometimes relegated to second place in the preoccupations of certain movements of the youth of Catholic Action.

The present crises of these movements—scouting in particular —illustrates the difficulty of being aware at one and the same time of the conditions which engender new needs in young people, and of the permanent values of education which must be preserved. The nerve center of the scouting crisis is the difficulty of reconcil-

[4] By "sexualism" is understood the exploitation of sexual ideas in all areas of human life.

ing young people's mutual desires and the unchangeable values of
personal education.

With the excuse of welcoming the aspirations of youth, do we
work with what causes them, flattering their weaknesses and
whims? Or do we propose that they exceed their limits and free
themselves of this conditioning? The whole problem is to know if,
at present, the development of the style of life which must be
envisaged in terms of mentalities is compatible with fidelity to a
proper pedagogy, primarily anxious to form the man.

It is repeatedly said that scouting would be more missionary in
character if it prepared boys to be men. That is true but insuffi-
cient. It is no less true that young people would be better prepared
to take charge of the world in which they live if they could give
back what they have received. Scouting will best fill its missionary
vocation by forming men who are competent, well-balanced and
open to others.

This task of educating the person and of awakening personal
liberty, far from being a stranger to the mission, seems, to the
contrary, one which it should assume with the greatest vigilance.
Faced with the alienation of the human person by the conditioning
of the masses, the humble task of the mission is to safeguard the
liberty of man by a triple means:

Recalling the Demands of Tolerance

Through the strength of equilibrium communicated by charity,
the Christian receives the mission and the grace to maintain a
harmony between the needs of openness in welcome and firmness
in truth.

Directing the Means to the Desired End

Our civilization, preoccupied with freeing man from the material servitude which endangers his liberty, runs the risk of enslav-
ing him by imposing means upon him as ends. It is sufficient to
mention, for example, the use of the automobile and television.
The Christian, recognizing that all good comes to him from God,
uses what the creator puts at his disposition without the proprie-

tary sense. Can he not give, through an evangelical detachment, the witness of availability which is the sign of liberty in the use of goods? It still remains for us to translate the imperatives of evangelical renunciation in terms of liberation and as the sign of a capacity for greater love.

Restoring the Meaning of the Human Person

Because man is made to be free, he cannot help but attempt unceasingly to climb out of his pit, if only on tiptoe. In his attempts to emerge, he always experiences the emergence of the values of his dignity. By the witness of his life, the Christian can make the man immersed in the world aware of the environment which enslaves him. Indicating to man the paths to liberty will help him to find himself. And among these roads, isn't one path the Gospel?

7 THE CHRISTIAN ENGAGED WITHIN THE STRUCTURES OF THE CITY

The Christian is a person seen by the world. His witness is the light he reflects. Witness is his serious concern to accept Christ's Word: "You are the light of the world."

In the heart of the world, the Christian is a person who is judged. Mixed in with other men, his human contacts are the salvation of his action; they are the realization of the words of the Lord: "You are the salt of the earth."

The Christian witness diffuses a light to the outside. His engagement, which gives consistency to his witness in authenticating it, shines from the Christian like a nucleus inside the atom.

Before approaching the question of engagement in the city structures, we should renew within ourselves the conviction that missionary action is inseparable from our strictly human tasks. When we speak of this task of man, we mean that the kingdom of God is constructed by the cooperation of men in completing the world. But we know that most of the time this task of man is confused with the work done every day to earn a living. It is the monotonous everyday work which constitutes the work of completing the world. It is through this work that the Christian participates in the construction of the kingdom. It is through the way in which this task is done that Jesus Christ is announced.

In the perspective of the construction of the kingdom through earthly work, we ascertain that the participation of the laity in the structures of the world is the privileged way for a Christian to announce the kingdom. But what does this participation entail? Is it even possible?

First of all, let us say this: When we speak of involvement in the structures, we must insist on the necessity, for the Christian who wishes to be a missionary, of participating in step with the world. The announcement of Jesus Christ supposes a preliminary work— to make the world susceptible to this announcement, open to the message. To be engaged in the structures means to hold a place in the world which will permit, on one level or another (professional, cultural, political), the possibility of opening it, of acting in its development.

To be engaged in the structures *as a Christian* means to explicitly want to hold that place in the world in sight of the kingdom; to want to arrange one's involvement in the world so as to prepare the world to welcome the kingdom; to want to shape the world so that, when completely fulfilled, it will one day become the Church.

But what makes the world develop? What directs the world? The world of men is ruled by a certain number of laws which we have already briefly analyzed: business, success, advancement, money, interest, competition, etc. It appears that the Christian must act at the level of these internal laws, the true dynamisms of the world. These laws are bearers, in a positive or negative way, of the human values, the soil in which the evangelical values capable of announcing Jesus Christ take root.

It is in leading the unbeliever to discover the values of justice, solidarity, unity among men, etc., as the very expression of the life of Christ, that he can be led to experience the person of Christ. That is why the believer must be particularly careful to help the unbeliever to make the connection between values and persons. It is through the lives of Christians in the world, living the values of the world as Christ would have lived them, that this connection is possible.

The life of the world, grasped by means of these values, is the raw material of missionary action. The missionary should take the experienced data of existence, which he shares in his work, as the point of application of his action. In this sense, the missionary role of the lay person entails extracting human values by giving them an evangelical consistency which becomes the full meaning of the sign of the kingdom. There is reconversion of the values of justice and solidarity into values of charity and hope that in turn become the source of the world's conversion. It is this reconversion which permits the unbeliever, concretely and vitally, to discover in acts the life of Christ.

But how is this conversion to be accomplished? Is it even possible? This is the whole question of the Christian's engagement in the structures. As we did with regard to the dialogue with unbelievers, we will recall, after the fashion of the psalmist, our distinction between the "involved" and the "uninvolved."

I
THE UNINVOLVED

By the uninvolved we mean the immense number of Christians who—aside from reasons of laziness, time or lack of faith—cannot participate because their position in society does not permit it—for example, the housewife, the small shopkeeper, the craftsman, the isolated office worker. We have said that involvement in the structures is possible only if we are in a position permitting direct contact with these structures. Most of these persons are unable to do this because they work apart, in an isolated way, without the possibility of entering into a sphere of influence.

To be sure, involvement in the structures is not limited solely to the possibilities of professional involvement. Some other structures exist at the social level and also at the levels of leisure and culture. Christians can have a real role, for example, in the PTA, planning committees and city councils. It is up to them to grasp this involvement with an eye on the kingdom of God.

II
THE INVOLVED

By the involved we do not mean those who belong to an elevated class of society, but simply those who, whether directing or directed, participate in a group and therefore have an effective role in the city. It is conceivable, of course, that the isolated worker who does not submit to his condition may belong as much to this category as his boss.

1. The Directing Classes

These are composed of politicians, economists, urban developers, civil servants, the world of employers and the professions in general—in a word, all those who have a certain influence upon the course of events in society.

A participating Christian should translate the Christian message by the way in which he conducts his affairs, by the manner in which he reacts to ambiguous situations, and by the strength of character he shows to safeguard his liberty in the midst of his work—that is, by his refusal to subordinate his faith to the interest of his employer. This manner of living implies a certain number of exigencies of action and moral qualities.

(a) *Exigencies of Action*

The Christian's involvement cannot thrive on a strictly personal level; it cannot be isolated. It demands a concerted action, a concentration of efforts, an organization. It implies combat. How can the Christian participate in the action of other Christians in the world who are similarly involved?

It seems that, on the professional level, a syndical action would permit the Christian in these directing classes to act effectively. This cooperative effort presents the risk of becoming an end in itself. If it becomes exclusive, it is liable to get lost in the impasse of progressivism, which errs in wanting to humanize first and then evangelize. There is the danger of constructing the terrestrial city and losing sight of the goal pursued—that of the kingdom. To avoid this danger, the Christian's engagement in the world demands a perpetual revision of the dynamics of his action, in the light of the Gospel.

That is the task of Catholic Action. It helps engaged Christians to recenter the objectives at which they aim, in their struggle in the world, on the final objective: the kingdom. It is a necessity for the Christian missionary who wants to evangelize the world through the place which he occupies in society and to compare the objectives of his struggle with those who, like him, are concerned with the kingdom of God.

Catholic Action, regrouping the militants according to their life environment, helps them all to reflect as teams on the difficulties each encounters in the place where he carries on his combat alone. The engagement of Catholic Action consists of viewing as a team, and in the mirror of the Gospel, one's action in the light of the kingdom. Let us make it clear that this engagement does not constitute a second engagement superimposed upon that of the militant in the city. It is because he is engaged in the world for the kingdom that the Christian engages himself in Catholic Action. It is the same engagement.

(b) *Moral Qualities*

Some qualities are natural, such as unselfishness, integrity and solidarity. These are pre-missionary qualities. They constitute a manner of being which should pass over into acts and express itself by taking a position. For example, a Christian who has responsibilities in the management of a business should try to orient the decisions to be taken in terms of the human factors they involve.

An objection can be raised: "It isn't necessary to be a Christian to be concerned for human values and the welfare of people. A non-Christian employer could watch over and foresee the human consequences of decisions he makes about working conditions."

That is true. However, the Christian, as opposed to the man who acts through altruism, acts through the love of Christ, a love expressed in the decisions he makes. And it is this love with which he views things which is itself the proclamation of the message. To be sure, a further objection could be made: "You are foundering in utopia! If you believe a Christian employer can act in an unselfish way, without being influenced by the interests of his business, and if you think that his witness can be received as a message of love, you're not being realistic."

The realism of the Christian militant is that of a man who recognizes, according to the logic of the world, that utopia and who converts it into a real hope. It is precisely because, in the eyes of the world, the Christian sees the outlines of that utopia and knows its cause, that he announces Jesus Christ according to hope. It is that perseverance in living according to the laws of the kingdom—judged utopian by the world but lived in hope—which enables the Christian to bear the values of the kingdom and, consequently, to announce the kingdom.

This is the total teaching of St. Paul: "What is madness in the eyes of the world is wisdom in the eyes of God." The message of Christ himself was received by the incredulous as a scandal. To want to be rid of this madness, this scandal, is to renounce Jesus Christ crucified. It is by throwing light on this contradiction of the world with the Gospel that the crucified and risen Christ is announced today. The value of the missionary announcement should not be judged on the fruit it bears in the world of unbelief. What is important is not the response the world gives, but the way the Christian announces. Just because a Christian is accused of being an idealist, his announcement cannot be judged *ipso facto* null and void.

The class struggle is another example which shows how specifically Christian love, poured into the heart of the struggle, can announce the kingdom. Marxists consider the class struggle as a privileged means of worker combat, and provoke and seek it for itself. The Christian knows that it is only an inevitable consequence of the present day which must be endured while trying to reduce its effects.

The message of social justice carried by a Marxist is different from the witness of justice borne by a Christian seeking to live as a child of God. The Christian is not one who refuses to struggle; he is one who refuses to conduct warfare as the world does. It is thus in bringing out, on the level of witness, the motivation of his behavior that the Christian can announce the kingdom by his attitude in the struggle. The fact of being obliged to accept the struggle, and at the same time refusing to conduct it with hate, is itself the announcement of the kingdom of God.

2. The Directed Classes

In this category are all those who belong in one way or another to the ongoing working world. It is the world of the employee. All that we have just said about the Christian's behavior when engaged in the directing classes is obviously applicable to Christians engaged in the directed classes. There we find the same exigencies of moral order and concerted action.

Again, it is syndicalism which seems the best response to that necessity of cohesion in action. It is perhaps imposed in a stronger manner in the directed classes, because the Christian isolated in the masses has less possibility of making himself heard than the

Christian acting in the directing classes. This basic syndicalist action possesses a harder character than it does with the directing classes, because it develops in an atmosphere of class struggle and needs. However, the role of syndicates must not be limited to the aspect of struggle, since the primary role of syndicalism is the representation of professions.

It is through this thirst for justice, among other things, that the Christian engaged in combat announces the kingdom of God. We are obliged to recognize that this thirst for justice is quenched at its source to the detriment of those who would seek to show it. That is why the combat for justice is carried out in confrontation with the world of directing classes. It is liable to develop into a struggle which opposes Christians of one class with Christians of the other.

The activity of Christians engaged in this combat can sink into social struggle for itself. The Christian might be tempted to confuse the advent of the kingdom of God with the pursuit of his interests. Like the militant of the directing classes, the militant of the directed classes should feel the need to authenticate his motives for action. Such is the role of Catholic Action.

III

CONCLUSION

*Conditions Required for the Christian's Engagement
To Be of Missionary Value*

From all that has been said, it is clear that it is not confrontation as such, but the evangelical contents with which the confrontation is filled, that constitutes the announcement. A dual condition seems to be necessary for that engagement to bear the Gospel content:

1. The Christian, who is fully in the world, should accept all the consequences of the world's struggle and his insertion in the struggle.

2. Because that struggle is carried on in the world in view of the kingdom, the Christian should seek to disengage himself from the "world," narrowly speaking. He is in the world but he is not of the world, in the sense that he does not live according to worldly logic. He makes use of the world as if he did not use it. The mission-

ary value of his engagement depends on the way in which he disengages himself from that worldly logic to reveal the logic of the Gospel.

In order for the Christian's engagement in the world to have value as a sign of the kingdom, it must be the expression both of an authentic attachment to the world and of a capacity to detach himself from the world. It is that capacity of detachment from the world which manifests a world beyond the world: the kingdom. It is this dialectic—attachment-detachment, engagement-disengagement—which is properly missionary, revealing that love which is specifically Christian, the only one capable of revealing the person of Christ through life.

This "detachment" is not the false freedom achieved by retreating from the conflict. Nor is it the spiritual attitude of one who relies blindly on the will of the Lord. It is essentially a question of the objectivity of the believer who, after considering the realities of the world and of the kingdom according to their irreducible order, makes his word the Word of the Lord: "I do not pray that thou take them out of the world, but that thou keep them from evil" (Jn. 17, 15-16).

In brief, we can say that it is just as important to speak of the disengagement as it is to speak of the engagement of the Christian with the world. The Christian mixes with the men of his time, not to be confused with them but rather to be the flavor of life. He is put into the world not to settle into it but to have the material of life which permits him to extract from all human values the seeds of the Gospel, the fruit of which is love. It is only if the motives behind this engagement are of a supernatural order that the Christian can announce the kingdom. It is the love of the kingdom, present in the heart of the struggle, that announces the kingdom itself.

Engagement with the World and Opening to the World

The idea of engagement implies an opening to the world. We often speak of that opening to the world with candor and facility. It is fairly easy if it is only a question of being smilingly receptive to the values of the world. As long as we remain at the stage of a general consideration of the necessity of opening to the world, this opening is viewed as a need to sympathize, and that seems to go without saying.

However, to be open to the world is to come into contact with the world. This contact is often violent, for it takes place in confrontation with the real. This contact produces a shock. If it does not, it is because the work of the Christian in the world does not collide with the world's resistance. The missionary, who wants to encounter the world in order to communicate the Christian message to it, should know that this opening must be made broad and deep and not selective. In order to open to the world, the world must be entered. The Church which opens to the world enters the heart of the world's wound.

To announce Jesus Christ to the interior of the world means to save the world as Christ saved it in taking upon himself all the sins of the world. This entails a certain number of requirements on the part of those who are not actively engaged in the world.

It is an evasion to use, as a pretext for doing nothing, the corruption of the world. It is evident, for example, that political life is not very clean. But to withdraw from this domain will not improve it. It is up to the Christian to purify it. Likewise, with regard to the labor movement, it is easy to use its possible political ends as an excuse to ignore it and take no part. There, again, the Christian must participate within it.

We have deplored the fact that many unbelievers judge the faith of the Church by the sins and caricatures of Christians. But also we see a goodly number of Christians who underestimate their ability to penetrate the world and who judge politics and syndicalism according to the deviations.

From a more moral point of view, a set purpose of kindness is required in meeting the actual world. It is evident that many Christian militants wear themselves out in battle, make errors and become impassioned or bitter. Confronted with the slow progress of the struggle and mediocre results, it is essential to consider free of condescension those who give of themselves, sometimes to the extent of giving their lives.

8 THE TEST OF CHRISTIAN INSTITUTIONS

Having determined the criteria which allow us to judge the missionary value of every action, we should seek what conditions are needed to assemble the constituting elements of missionary action. This raises the whole question of *Christian institutions*.

I

THE INSTITUTIONAL CHURCH
AND INSTITUTIONS OF THE CHURCH

1. The Preliminaries

In a general way, what is meant by institution? Missionary action, which approaches reality in the multiplicity of its aspects, supposes the determination of means to be taken in terms of the immediate aims pursued. Whatever its limitations, missionary action presupposes organization, which takes form through the device called "institution." It is thus, for example, that the evangelization of the working class is assumed by the Young Christian Workers, an organization which tries to adapt its methods and means in terms of the environment.

Is the mission bound to institutions? Some Christians have the impression that they are smothering under the weight of institutions which seem to paralyze their action. Because of the complexity of these institutions, which of itself creates a considerable waste of energy, many people prefer autonomy in action.

Even if the merits of certain institutions can be questioned, the principle of institutional action cannot be questioned. For one thing, the institution is itself the product of action, and for another, to reject institutional life as such would be to reject the Church. The problem, therefore, is to know what qualities should enhance institutions that they might fulfill their function as servants of action.

2. The Church, Mother of Institutions

The Church, in herself, is fundamentally institutional, but an institution not founded by human will. The Church is instituted by Jesus Christ. The Church, desired as such by Christ, is of divine institution.

The institutional character of the Church is inherent in her nature. The Church is a structured body: the body of Christ, possessing a head and members. The Church, like all bodies, is organized, with a set purpose and function.

The institutional character of the Church is inherent in the nature of the goal she pursues: to communicate salvation to all men living in this world in structured society. Rejoining the world, the Church communicates salvation institutionally. The means she proposes—Word, sacraments, community—constitute the fundamental institution *par excellence,* called the "ecclesial institution."

3. The Institutions of the Church

(a) *The Internal Life of the Church: The Ecclesiastical Institutions.* If Christ himself chose Word, sacraments and community as providential means of salvation, he wanted equally to leave men free to organize—with the assistance of the Holy Spirit—the mobilizing of these means. He instituted the sacraments and left it up to the Church to administer them the way she understood them —hence the role of the liturgy, to which he fixed no rubric. These means which the Church takes to organize her internal life are called "ecclesiastical institutions."

Among the ecclesiastical institutions, we can include the liturgy, dioceses, parishes, seminaries, religious orders, catechism and catechumenate, etc. Ecclesiastical institutions embody in time and space the ecclesial institution, pouring it into the culture of the people and adapting it to the needs of local communities.

The Church as such is the Word of eternal life. The Church as an institution is immovable. But the ecclesiastical institutions which express the ecclesial institution are fleeting, perishable, adaptable and transformable. Whatever the Church does, she can undo; whatever she gives birth to, she can bury. Thus, for example, reforming the liturgy is not changing religion, whereas changing the Gospel or the sacraments would be really changing the Church. Changing the way in which the sacraments are given is not changing the institutional Church, but rather adapting the institutions of the Church.

From the missionary point of view, what can we expect from the ecclesiastical institutions? Certain institutions are, of themselves, missionary—for example, the catechumenate. Others are missionary in terms of the spirit animating them—for example, the parishes. Still others cannot be missionary by their very nature—for example, the liturgy. The mission is sent outside. We cannot demand that the liturgy be missionary, since it develops "inside" and for the Christian community. The liturgy is not missionary just because a passing unbeliever in a church is touched by grace at the moment of liturgical celebration. Just because Paul Claudel was converted at Notre Dame during a midnight Mass, it cannot be deduced that the liturgy at Notre Dame is missionary in nature or orientation.

(b) *The Church in Her Relations with the World: Christian Institutions.* The missionary dialogue of the Church with the world takes shape in the meeting of the institutions of the world and the institutions of the Church. The meeting place is Christian institutions. By Christian institutions we mean all the institutions which draw their reason for being from the kingdom of God.

Some justify themselves by the desire to construct the human city according to a certain Christian vision of the world—for example, the Christian political parties or the Christian unions. Others pursue more directly the objective of the kingdom through the mediation of human tasks which involve the Church in the city—for example, the Christian school. These Christian institutions are called "temporal." Among these temporal institutions should be distinguished "purely temporal institutions" and "confessional institutions."

By *purely temporal institutions* we mean those which confer upon the Church power in the city—that is, in the management of political, economic and social affairs. These purely temporal institutions structured the theocratic power of the Church. They flourished after Constantine and Charlemagne during the most beautiful epoch of Christianity, when it was not wrong to say that Christ was king of France!

The golden age of temporal institutions is over. They could not resist the assaults of history, popular movements and revolutionary assassinations. "The late Christianity," Emmanuel Mounier said of that age. But if times have changed, certain old mentalities have petrified in a conservatism represented by the integrist tendency. Is it necessary, from the missionary point of view, to judge the values of these temporal institutions?

It should be enough to consider the regime of Franco and the manner in which the film *To Die in Madrid* stigmatized the Spanish Civil War to realize the world's unbelieving judgment. We can dispense with any commentary and simply say that it seems good that these temporal "Christian" institutions can do nothing more than bear counter-witness. Doesn't the pope's *de facto* renunciation of temporal power, accepted at least after the event, confirm the Church's need to detach herself from any form which might be judged imperialistic by the world?

By *confessional institutions* we mean all temporal institutions which exist by reason of the desire of the Church to help Christians live in a secularized world according to the demands of a faith which is, according to Fr. Liégé, "totalizing with regard to all experiences of human life."

Constructing in the world a world for Christians, these confessional institutions revive the institutions of the city by finalizing them in a Christian way. School is always school. But through the Christian school, Christians claim to carry out the job of Christian education. As compared with purely temporal institutions, these confessional institutions are presented modestly, like servants. They do not necessarily pursue an immediate religious goal. As a direct objective, they are given the task of human education.

In the domain of youth, they act through the instrumentality of schools, youth centers, various movements, and sporting and cultural associations. These are *educative* confessional institutions.

In the social domain, they act through the instrumentality of works of kindness and solidarity: nursing homes, missions in slums, care for the elderly, etc. These are *charitable* confessional institutions.

In the domain of civil life, they act through the mediation of political and social action in which Christians can play a specific role, conforming to the doctrine of the Church. That is the job of Christian parties, Christian labor unions, and Christian social secretariats. These are the confessional institutions which we term as *engaged* and which best correspond to what we have said about the Christian involved in the structures.

From the missionary point of view, what is the value of these confessional institutions? To the extent that they help Christians to open themselves to the world and display the Church's interest in life's contingent realities, they help establish a sympathetic *rapport* which can be the beginning of a more profound dialogue. To the extent that they consist simply of rendering service in an evangelical way, they contribute to announcing, in acts, the charity of Christ. However, this witness is not free of ambiguity. For Christians, there is the danger of establishing cozy groups who oppose the world with their self-complacency. In the world of unbelief, there is the danger that the witness of charity will be judged as equivalent to philanthropy.

II

THE TEST OF CHRISTIAN INSTITUTIONS

The risks and dangers which we just briefly mentioned include a set of grievances against Christian institutions which should be examined objectively.

1. The Viewpoint of the Unbelieving World

Regarded from the angle of institutions, the world in which we live is characterized by three phenomena: socialization, democratization and secularization. What we call "mass strength" is magnified. Public opinion is determined by all those slogans it nourishes that put it on guard against everything which might interfere with the security of secularism. Fear of dictatorship in any form, thirst for free thought and obsession with neutrality excite a laicism which is expressed by a fierce demand for liberty, opposing everything that might threaten constraint.

The Church faces this mentality with the passivity she assumed in the epoch of Christianity when she occupied a dominant position. The world of unbelief still judges the Church of today on the misdeeds of the Church of yesterday. It is impossible to talk with the unbeliever without his reserving the warmed-over, but real, dishes of the Inquisition, the Renaissance popes, the Galileo affair, etc. In other words, the world still mistrusts the Church and interprets her right to have institutions as a brooding will for power, a temptation to usurp power.

2. The Viewpoint of the Christian in the World

The Christian, anxious to establish contact between the Church and the world, notes these complaints and fears, and he tries to reconcile the dual necessity of belonging to an institution in order to be effective, and of disengaging himself from that institution because it might be wrongly judged.

How, then, are we to take into consideration both the mentality of the world of unbelief and the need to institutionalize?

3. Renunciation

What permits us to pass beyond and emerge from the dialectic of "attachment-detachment" is the Church's capacity for renunciation. The Church presents herself to the world with the declared intention of being the servant of the poor. This declaration can be taken seriously by the world only if the Church decides to make herself poor. This means knowing how to be detached from all that is not essential in order to be enriched by what will permit the world to receive her.

What does this renunciation consist of?

(a) Renunciation of that conquering proselytism whose characteristic is to act with striking force, with the spirit of the Crusades. It is not because we refuse to make a public display that we have human respect. Witness is true when it is interior. It penetrates because of the evangelical quality of its motives and its contents and not because of the labels with which we mask our title and our behavior. It is in this spirit that some groups believe they should "deconfessionalize" themselves. This is not the place to say if this is right or not, but it seems that these decisions are taken in view of the mentality of the world of unbelief, which interprets as propaganda what in fact is the simple recognition of who we are.

(b) Renunciation of everything which is an external sign of wealth. This assures the institution of its foundation and makes triumphalism and paternalism less likely.

(c) Renunciation of civil functions which were often the *raison d'être* of many institutions. Until the Revolution, the Church in France maintained the national registries; she owned and operated most of the hospitals and directed the biggest colleges.

4. The Qualities of an Institution

Institutions serving the Church (which herself serves the world) should never set themselves up as being absolute, at the risk of engendering a spirit of competition or monopoly. Essentially contingent, they should know how to stand aside when they have served their purpose. The misfortune in the Church results because the promises of the continuous character of the ecclesial institution are applied to Christian institutions. When new institutions are born, they must be given their notice of decease, and an age limit should be fixed. Otherwise, they will be condemned to live years of lethargy after their years of activity have long ceased. It is also necessary to avoid institutionalizing experiences which can only be passing.

Before promoting an awakening of faith and the education of charity, Christian institutions should themselves be true and exigent. They should not be allowed to bypass the goal which they propose, nor be used for things other than that for which they were created. Consider, for example, the schools. Very often, recruitment in our good liberal arts colleges is dependent upon the financial status of the students, and the students very often belong to a world where faith is, if not dead, at least a purely sociological phenomenon. This could be the terrain where the Christian school might have its purpose, promoting the mission in the so-called "independent" groups.

To promote the opening of the Church to the world, Christian institutions should encourage the entrance of Christians into the structures of the world. To that end, they should avoid keeping the best Christians of the community for internal use and for weak missionary yield.

To avoid any ambiguity and to retain every liberty of expression and research, Christian institutions should support Christians engaged in the various structures, and they should be autonomous with regard to the world and the hierarchy. They should not be politically aligned—for example, the labor unions should not presume to indicate the position of the Church—but should maintain freedom of choice. To link the Church to a faction is to cripple her universality.

To promote the opening of the Church to the world, Christian institutions should never be hostile to other institutions, even if such institutions seem to neutralize those of the Church. The safe-keeping of the Christian's essential liberties must be respected. In defending his liberties, the Christian should not make the world think that he is defending himself in order to oppose the world, but rather that he demands with respect to faith what the world itself demands in its lack of faith—namely, freedom.

III

Conclusion

If it were necessary, in a few words, to sum up the role which should be filled by Christian institutions in the missionary Church, the following postulate could be set forth: The purpose of Christian institutions is to encourage evangelization by permitting it to penetrate the cultural and sociological phenomena which mark our times. But having set forth the postulate, the question rebounds. Haven't Christian institutions in fact neutralized the Christian mission? If we consider the history of the mission, what does it teach us?

Since the Word is compared in the bible to a sword, we might say that the mission, in the era of the primitive Church, was at the *iron age,* piercing through hearts and turning them inside out. The Church, with few structures, was concerned only to proclaim the Word, to transmit faith and to effect conversion. Everything was centered upon the edification of the community of living stones.

As the history of the mission was engaged in time, after Charlemagne and following Constantine, the *stone age* appeared. The Church constructed basilicas, shrines, seminaries, schools and hospitals. In doing this, she stratified herself by petrifying into institutions which became ends in themselves.

In the 17th century (that of the theology of the Counter-Reformation which put the accent on the visible character of the Church by insisting on her hierarchical organization), the primary objective of the mission seems to have been the implantation of the visible Church. To be a missionary was to be a pioneer and to install the Church sociologically in strong and stable structures.

We can understand the primacy given—if not in intention, at least in action—to the desire to root the Church as a visible society. In order to receive the unbelievers called to faith, it is necessary to receive them into a community able to nourish their faith. But the preoccupation with creating the framework often engenders the danger of neglecting the contents.

As regards the mission, it seems that this danger has not been avoided. Canon Boulard has said that many regions have been Christianized sociologically without having been, in the correct sense, evangelized—that is, without having been summoned by the Word and called to conversion. Why?

Since Christian institutions were tied up historically with the institutions of the city, the mission was fossilized in temporal structures; the Church was confused with the State. Let us consider how the mission might have been conceived of in the 5th century. In 496, Clovis was baptized. As chief of the temporal city, he brought with him the Franks, who became, all at the same time, the Church of France. Let us also remember Charlemagne who made conversion campaigns the way wars are made.

We should have the courage now to let old institutions die in order to create those which are truly and specifically missionary. If it is not Catholic Action or special missions like the Mission of France, what missionary devices do we have in France?

After the age of iron and the age of stone, we enter perhaps into that *age of fire* about which St. John the Baptist says: "He will baptize you with the Holy Spirit and with fire. His winnowing fan is in his hand, and he will thoroughly clean out his threshing floor, and will gather his wheat into the barn, but the chaff he will burn up with unquenchable fire" (Mt. 3, 12).

In the hand of Christ we are that winnowing fan. He expects us to set on fire all these outdated institutions which we value perhaps because we value ourselves who love them. It is this purifying fire which will permit us to receive the harvest of the work in the storehouse of the Church—namely, the fire of which Christ spoke and which should be burning in us: "I have come to cast fire upon the earth, and what will I but that it be kindled?" (Lk. 12, 49). It is within us that Christ burns with this desire, for this fire is love. Love can succeed in the world only if it is lighted in the home of charity, which is the Church. Only a love worthy of the hearts of men can bring life to Christian institutions.

9 PARISH AND MISSION

If it were necessary to put Christian institutions to the test one by one, it seems likely that the parish would be found in the first rank of the accused. Summarizing the classic grievances of those who have already judged it without appeal, the parish—at least the urban parish such as we know it in Paris—is becoming an anachronism. It can no longer answer the needs of the present situation. Why? It is disoriented by:

(a) the mobility of the population. People work, eat, sleep and amuse themselves in different places (consider, for example, the phenomenon of the weekend). The parish is no longer the place to gather.

(b) the instability of the population, resulting from frequent transfers and moving of households. The parish is no longer the place of family traditions.

(c) the scattering of modes of relations, established more at the level of class than of place. The parish is a superstructure.

In this situation, can the parish be a missionary instrument adapted to our times? Doesn't it unduly absorb the energies of the priests and the laity to the detriment of a missionary effort to penetrate the classes? Is it, for example, reconcilable with Catholic Action and the like?

The usual reaction of the pastor is defensiveness. If you question the pastors of Paris, they all have different ideas, according to who they are, what they do, and what parish they have inherited. The present pastor of St. Jean de Montmartre, former pastor of Saint-Severin, full of faith and hope in the parish, said: "The parish is missionary to the extent that it is open, receptive, and radiant."

The present rector of the seminary of the Mission of France, former pastor of Saint-Sulpice, full of benevolence for the parish, is reported to have said: "What I demand of the parish is that it not keep me from being a missionary!"

As for the present pastor of Saint-Pierre and Saint-Paul d'Ivry,

101

it appears that, on the day of his installation, he posted on his church door this sign: "Closed for reasons of evangelization!"

I

HISTORY AND DEFINITION

1. *Origin.* The word "parish" comes from the Greek *par-oiken*. *Oiken* means to live; *para* specifies that it concerns living in the neighborhood, here and there. The parish, then, designates all those who live in the same territory.

In the New Testament, St. Paul uses this word *par-oiken* (1 Cor. 1, 2) to designate the local communities to whom he speaks. Writing to the Corinthians, he uses the phrase "the church of God at Corinth." The term *par-oiken,* which we transcribe by the word "parish," indicates, in the New Testament, what we today call a diocese, which is the basic community of the Church, the parish being only a cell reduced to the dimension of the neighborhood.

In the history of the Church, the parish appears belatedly. It was the evangelization of countries which was the origin of the creation of parishes, the diocese having become much too spread out and scattered. It was only in the 9th century, under Charlemagne, that the territorial definition of parishes developed, not with a pastoral aim but for reasons of the nation, to facilitate the raising of tithes and to provide the constant access of the means of grace. In 1563, the Council of Trent obliged the parishes to be defined by attaching to them a resident pastor.

There are several types of parishes: territorial parishes, parishes for rites (for example, Saint-Julien-le-Pauvre, for the Greek Catholic), national parishes (for example, the Polish church in Paris), and family parishes. There are also "elected parishes," the existence of which is not legally recognized but which certainly exist in fact.

2. *Definition.* The purpose of a parish is to give, as Fr. Liégé says, "a visible expression to the community of the sanctified." To the extent that the parish expresses the mystical body of Christ, it can be defined in these terms: "The home of Christian animation which gives body to the baptized community, in assembling them by the Word and the eucharist, that they might live in the charity of Christ."

The juridical point of view is more precise, holding that the parish is an ecclesiastical institution of clerical order. The method of government of the parish is personal. It rests upon the person of the leader, and the leader is the pastor. We are perhaps shocked, in our very democratized mentality, by this monarchical form of institution, but it is best to know that this is what it is.

II

PERSONS AND INSTITUTIONS

1. The Legal and Factual Situation

(a) *The Clergy.* It is the pastor, who is responsible according to Canon Law, for the *cura animarum* or the care of souls. He is responsible for the parish, pastorally and administratively. He has full authority over the lay people and the assistants. These last-mentioned are named directly to the parish by the bishop to do a job sometimes attached to a precise function (for example, the curate occupied with marriages), or else determined by the pastor (for example, chaplain to the young people). The assistants are under the immediate authority of the pastor, with whom they share pastoral responsibilities and duties. But it is upon the bishop that they depend in the final instance.

(b) *Lay People.* The lay people surrounding the pastor are the support of the clergy. This expression indicates the state of dependence in which lay people collaborate. Properly speaking, they exercise diaconates—that is, they render services as the deacons did in the primitive Church. On the level of responsibility in the parish, they are not precisely what we could call "shareholders of the parochial society." At the very most, they are, in the present conception of the parish, *auxiliaries.* Even if they fill important offices which involve their personal responsibility and that of the parish (for example, as members of an administrative committee managing the budget), it is not the written code of the institution which confers full authority upon them; rather, it is the bishop who accords them this right. It is the pastor who summons the lay people. He chooses those who seem to him most suitable for duties in the parish. He can, without warning, remove those duties from them.

But, on the other hand, lay people can themselves—depending upon their wishes, and at any moment—withdraw or hand in their resignation, for they are acting as volunteers to give service. They have a consultative role when they perform a pastoral function on the level of works or the liturgy. They are entitled to speak and vote only if the pastor grants them this power and on condition that the clergy ratify their decisions.

All those who deplore this sort of relation, which keeps the laity in a state of subordination with regard to the clergy, must acknowledge it as a state of fact, the law of which is written into the institution. Considering this state of fact, how can we be surprised to note so many setbacks in attempts to achieve priest-laity collaboration? Is it astonishing to note so many dead parishes? If lay people refused to live hidden under the bushel basket, perhaps pastors would be more luminous and alive. And if the pastors truly enlightened lay people, perhaps the number of militants would not shrink to that of such a weak minority.

2. Future Situation

Facing this reality, it is not a matter of opposing the law but of knowing how to be faithful to the purpose of the parochial institution. Without pretending to bypass that institution, it is possible to bypass the letter; it is necessary to regain the spirit of the ecclesial institution. The essential thing is to assemble the People of God in a dynamic way so that they can put into practice the words of the Gospel: "In this is my Father glorified, that you may bear very much fruit, and become my disciples" (Jn. 15, 8).

How can God's people be educated to "do good not only before God but before men"? The institution must favor the creation of authentic communities in which responsibilities, shared by priests and lay people, permit them to operate effectively together.

It is not enough for community parishes to give witness of a real understanding between priests and lay people. An explicit desire is still necessary on the part of the clergy to create parochial communities where the lay responsibilities shared with the priests are not fictitious and not arranged exclusively for the material and inner organization of the parish.

It must be said that the dialogue between priests and lay people is not situated essentially at the level of a reciprocal understanding, but rather at the level of a mutual engagement. Engagement means responsibility. The primary role of the parish, from the missionary point of view, is to form lay people to assume responsibilities.

Finally, if we recognize that the sacraments of baptism and confirmation confer upon lay people a right to assume responsibilities in the mission, how can the parish pretend to send into an unbelieving world Christians who are adult from the point of view of missionary action, but who are considered on the inside almost like minors? How can the desire to urge lay people to a full and active role in the world be taken seriously when they have no such role in the community? That active role of the laity in the parish is the prize not only of the parish but of the mission. It is the prize of the parish because it is the prize of the mission.

If it is admitted that a parish can live only to the extent that the lay people are directed toward those outside, and if, at the same time, it is recognized that lay people are at the heart of the mission, this bond of continuity between parish and mission appears quite clearly. There must be a correlation between the activities of each so that each may become more fruitful.

We can sum up the missionary vocation of the parish by this double paradox: no missionary parish without an "exteriorized clergy"; no missionary parish without an "interiorized laity." "Exteriorized" indicates a clergy stimulated by a laity, who, from the world's level, will inform, disturb and help the priests to get out of their parochial confines where internal preoccupations prevent them from being available to the world. "Interiorized" indicates a laity enlightened, nourished and supported by a priestly community which unceasingly reminds the actively engaged laity of the evangelical exigencies of the kingdom.

III
PRIESTS AND LAY MISSIONARIES WITHIN THE PARISH

The conception which we have of priest-laity collaboration in the parish is related to actual positions of priest-laity theology, to present pastoral conditions, and to the situation of the priest and the lay person in the world and in the Church. It is important, then, in the light of the analysis made of the situation of the lay person in the parish compared with that of the priest, to step back a bit in order to examine the consequences provoked by such a situation in mission material and to better discover the causes of lay inertia in the mission.

Traditionally, the priest is considered as the spiritual man and the lay person as the temporal man. Animator of the Christian community and the mission, the priest's specific domain of action is clearly defined: prayer, worship, sacraments, intellectual work, teaching, and collective and personal contacts. Ministry demands a great availability. The priest should be relieved of all material servitude hindering that which is exclusively expected of him.

Who is expected to assume these material services if not the lay person? But is this really the role of the laity? It is absolutely necessary to be aware of a generalized anomaly which consists of relying on the lay person for material things, with the pretext that he is, by his way of life, the temporal man.

When it is said that the lay person is the temporal man, it means that his natural insertion in the world enables him to act evangelically on its structures. When it is said that the lay person takes charge of the material affairs of a parish, it means that, at a pragmatic level, he takes care of the ongoing questions of operation. This reduction of "temporal" to "material" contributes to conceiving of the laity's mission as a job of servant to the priest.

It must be seen that this misconception of temporal as material is the immediate consequence of that more profound opposition between the spiritual and the temporal. This opposition would not lead to a missionary impasse if it expressed the priest-lay person distinction which must be made from baptism rather than from a hierarchical pyramid conception which places the priest at the summit and the lay person at the bottom. In this perspective, the missionary role of the lay person should be considered to be just as important as that of the priest, because it is the expression of a unique baptism.

It would be rather abnormal, with the excuse of freeing the priest of material tasks, to overburden the lay person with all the jobs which would keep him from fulfilling his mission in the world. It would be just as serious to keep a lay person busy in the parish when he might be a missionary in the world as it would be to monopolize a priest in activities outside his spiritual ministry. Since the priest is irreplaceable in his ministry and the lay person is irreplaceable in the world, there should be an exchange of equally divided responsibilities.

On the other hand, taking into account what we have just affirmed and at the risk of appearing to contradict ourselves, we can say that taking charge of material affairs belongs to the laity, in fact if not by right. Too many lay people who render service to the parish imagine that they are rendering service to the priests. It is not for the priests that the laity act. They are not fix-it mechanics for pastors. They are active members of a community; it is they who make the parish live. Even though their participation in the parochial community may be essentially voluntary, unpaid, and often expressed with a devotion surpassing that of many priests, it must be said again that this self-sacrifice, demanded by the very nature of the community, is derived as much from justice as from charity.

The levels would undoubtedly be much more distinct if lay people were not regarded in the parish in an almost paternalistic fashion. Concerning the material administration of the parish, it would be desirable that the priest-laity collaboration be made without ambiguity on the professional level. Rather than begging everyone everywhere for compulsory unpaid services, why not hire, when finances permit it (and they do more often than is thought), professional people with competence for missionary tasks.

Thus, in our parochial community, some secretaries are employed full time. Some staff members also have regular, paid functions: recreational aides, service personnel, sacristans, etc. Along these same lines, why not envisage permanent employees who will fill in a functional way, and with professional competence, such posts as organizers and bookkeepers? The regular, paid cooperation assures continuity in services, clarity in relations and, above all, efficiency in action. What a gain this would be from the missionary point of view, because many more lay people would be much more available.

Therefore, it is in this Church spirit, where the members are bound together to fill individually a set function, that parochial life must be viewed if we want it to be efficacious from a missionary point of view.

To the question of mission are attached numerous questions

which appear annexed—for example, finances. In the parishes, is the budget run in terms of missionary needs? That would be saying a lot.[1] Missionary concern should inform the way of conducting the parish at every level of parochial life.

Concluding the question of priests and lay people in the parish, we will content ourselves with two remarks:

(a) The lay person ought to be interested in pastoral life and keep informed about it by becoming cultivated religiously. However, he should avoid the temptation of wishing to perform the priest's work. In the matter of the liturgy, for example, he does not have enough competence to know what should be done. His role is not to quibble over a *Confiteor* to be removed or added but to inform the clergy of the feeling of the assembly so that the priests can reconcile the needs expressed by the faithful with the exigencies of pastoral life.

(b) Since the priest is the spiritual man, he should be consecrated to his task, according to the Word of the Lord himself: "And for them I sanctify myself, that they also may be sanctified in truth" (Jn. 17, 19). But he should remember that he is not a disincarnated spiritual man. He can take part in the lives of the men to whom he must transmit the life of God only if he is interested in their lives and participates in the contingencies and servitudes of existence. Thus, to take charge of certain material tasks in the midst of the parish is not opposed to the essential character of his ministry; indeed, there is no incompatibility in principle between material tasks and spiritual ministry.

The priest should not balk at some servitudes which may be imposed upon him by circumstances. But this incarnate spiritual ministry must not lead the priest into the same errors which the laity might commit. He must not interfere in the tasks which properly belong to lay people!

IV

No Parish without the Mission; No Mission without the Parish

The paradox which we seem to find between parish and mission will be removed when that clergy-laity opposition is abolished. The tension between parish and mission will be resolved by an interac-

[1] Cf. "Pastorale et Finances," in *Paroisse et Mission* 21.

tion which Fr. Le Sourd formulates in these terms: "The mission needs the parish; the parish needs the mission."

The Mission Needs the Parish

We have admitted that human relations are established more by class than by place, but it is incontestable that society will always be implanted on a territory and that it will be influenced by the life of the place. In this respect, the parish will always have a specific role to play. The question is not the role, but rather how to fill it. The parish should adapt itself, renew itself and find adequate means for filling its new functions in a changing world.

The Parish Needs the Mission

If it wishes to have a certain inner vitality, the parish must find it in breathing the fresh air from outside. The world of unbelief is like a stimulant forcing the parish to progress and to question itself. In this way, the world of unbelief contributes to the renewal of the parish.

What are the conditions required for a parish to be in a state of mission?

(a) *No Missionary Parish without the Missionary Team.* For that, the parish should play a relay role. It must be a turntable between Catholic Action and diverse missions like the Mission de France, the Latin Quarter Mission, diocesan missions, etc., which work on place and class at the same time. The parish can play this relay role only if it is aware of the missionary efforts of neighboring parishes. It was with this in mind that deaneries were created in Paris and sectors determined. A pilot parish acting independently could have at the most only the witness of a test pilot and not that of the Church. The world of unbelief awaits from the Church a concordant and universal witness.

(b) *Priority of Intention and Action toward Those Outside.* For a parish to be missionary, it must be turned resolutely toward the outside and, in the order of action, create missionary institutions. Which ones? There are not many. The Centre Pastoral des Missions à l'Intérieur permanently conducts, at the sociological level, an investigation of mentalities which allows the parish to be aware of the "environments" of pastoral action.

Within parishes, shouldn't it be urgent to create teams of lay people in charge of studying, from a missionary point of view, the problems posed by the penetration of a class or a neighborhood? Just as there are workshops for preaching, for the liturgy, etc., couldn't there be workshops for missionary study with more or less long-term action in mind?

The resolution to agree in intention and in action, with priority given to those outside, can be effective only if it is expressed in common study which engages the whole community through an experience undertaken at one point or another and judged severely in terms of the immediate objectives pursued.

(c) *Beyond Public Life, the Hidden Life.* The parish is missionary to the extent that it is open, receptive and radiant. But this openness and receptiveness demand long preliminary efforts of improvement and renovation which employ vital strengths. Numerous parishes which have given the example of these virtues of reception have, at the same time, drawn attention to a danger that must be avoided: namely, spending time in clearing away, cleaning, resurfacing, moving, installing and creating frameworks. All this work of putting into place is but a beginning.

As much as the demons of false piety and bad taste have been exercised, we still have not passed to the mission. As long as we remain tending parochial structures which permit the parish to live and open itself, we have made only the first step. We are at the stage where the Gospel tells us that the house is clean, swept, decorated and rid of its demons, but empty. That state, the Gospel tells us in a surprising manner, is worse than the first, for if the state of dirtiness engenders routine and blindness, the state of the brilliant façade engenders the temptation of satisfaction and self-admiration which rapidly sinks into the sin of self-complacency, withdrawal and closing within oneself. This is obviously the death of the mission.

After the preliminary work of reception, the parish must have the courage to give up its temptation to "perfectionism." It should, in all humility, tackle a work of depth based upon precise objectives which will perhaps not bear fruit immediately, because there is the law of the Gospel: "If the seed which falls into the ground does not die, it bears no fruit." When the seed falls into the ground and dies, we must still remember the golden rule of the missionary: "One man harvests what another has sown."

10 THE MISSION OF PLACE
The Neighborhood Mission

At the end of this series of lectures on the mission, the feeling we have is perhaps akin to the apprehension felt by the scholar who, at a certain moment, stops his investigations and passes from the stage of observation to that of experimentation.

What will the experience give? We have created hypotheses and drawn conclusions; we have recorded a certain number of statements, clarified evidence and acquired convictions. In brief, the theory is ready. Here we are in the corner. The work must be accomplished with an instrument at our disposal which we did not choose: the parish. We must be missionaries where we are, within the framework of parochial action, bound to the contingencies of the neighborhood as it is, the most passionate and the most distressing.

The cross formed by the two boulevards of our parish bears the names of two great saints. Michael and Germaine, slashing our neighborhood like a scar. On both sides, two more streets, two more scars, two more saints: Jacques de Compostelle and Andre des Arts, not counting Julian the Poor and Severin the Solitary.

This neighborhood is hardly a paradise. The street called the "Fishing Cat" reminds us that men, too, fish a lot. There is the house of prostitution across the street from the church. There are the cellars where drugs are sold and where money is lost. But that is perhaps not the most serious. There are also attics divided into so-called "maids' rooms" which are unfit to live in. There are also the lost men whose lives smell of the sewers.

A well-dressed world, an artistic world, a needy world, the intellectuals and the pseudo-intellectuals, the bohemians and the workers—all this world rushes through these arteries. All of Paris is contained in what is still only the "Saint-Severin village," with its little street stalls, its cafés, its chalets, its gossip and tales, its

111

steeples and its non-electric bells. This is the mission field. How does the parish envisage it?

I
PRINCIPLES OF ACTION

In this neighborhood, so rich and so poor, how can the Gospel be germinated in its richness and in its spirit of poverty?

The Neighborhood: Mission of the Parish

The idea of mission implies the idea of action, to be led toward an end to be attained in terms of certain means to be taken. The ultimate end toward which the parish is headed is the same finality of the Church: to assemble all men into one people. The immediate end which the parish should pursue is the Church's *raison d'être:* to constitute a human community which might be more and more the finished sketch of the assembly of God's people.

The Role of the Neighborhood Mission: To Be the Real Presence of the Community

How can the parish call to all the people of its territory and assemble them? We answer immediately that it can do so by a certain *mode of human presence*, the evangelical quality of which is likely to pose a question.

From that affirmation, two corollaries emerge:

(a) the Christian community can be present to the neighborhood only if it has a hold on the neighborhood;

(b) that human presence can only be fruitful if Christians together are animated by the concern to give to their presence an evangelical quality which has meaning.

The principle of the neighborhood mission is clear. The Christian must simultaneously *take charge* of the life of the Christian community and the life of the neighborhood. This "taking charge" is the expression of a certain fundamental way of being which the face of Moses can help us to understand—Moses, on Sinai, in an interceding attitude, praying with outstretched arms, carrying in his heart the exigencies of the love of God, carrying in his arms his hardhearted people. It is the attitude of every Christian missionary who takes upon him and within him the "concern of the Church."

II

ORGANIZATION OF MISSIONARY ACTION

1. The Coordinates of the Problem: Place, Class, Human Distances

In elementary sociology, we study the human reality constituting man living in society according to two dimensions: the vertical and the horizontal. The *idea of place* corresponds to the vertical dimension. Man is considered in his geographical condition—where he lives, where he dwells. The *idea of class* corresponds to the horizontal dimension. Man is perceived in his human relations, according to the groups to which he belongs and which constitute a sort of "community of destiny," in which all the members have the same habits, mentality and reflexes. Thus we will speak of the middle class, the worker class, the artisan class, etc.

It is difficult to specify all the criteria upon which are based the designation of belonging to a class. It seems that these criteria are tied up principally with the working world and the professions, but many other factors come into play (age, among others). We will talk about the world of the young which covers the middle class and workers alike. The specialization of techniques and the growing specificity of classes which it engenders heighten the idea of class.

To the idea of class is attached another idea, at once broader and more precise, which groups men by the same sociological class according to their insertion in the world and according to their culture. It is the idea of *human distance*. Thus, there is the world of technicians, the world of finance, the world of lay teachers, etc. It is obviously very important to know which class we are dealing with, because the type of missionary action is different according to the way men are considered in the web of their human conditionings.

The missionary action which we must exert within the parish is exerted upon the place. Our Christian community is outlined as a territory. It is this territory which is mission land. In this territory, all the layers of society and all the classes are represented. Therefore, the mission of place is inseparable from the mission of class. We have no intention either to confuse the two or to oppose them. They are not exclusive. Men living in society are perceived through these two realities of the sociological order: place and class.

The class mission is the prerogative of *specialized Catholic Action,* the essential task of which is the evangelization of the class by members of that class.

The mission of place belongs to *the parish,* whose essential task is the evangelization of place by place.

Between place and class there are all the interferences of life which Catholic Action tries to reconcile within the framework of parochial action and which might be called "human distances." Thus, the neighborhood is a galaxy of human distances. As its primary objective, the neighborhood mission should aim at the total appeal to the territory's inhabitants through that to which they are bound. It is a question of discerning the various "communities of destiny" which assemble them.

These communities can be discerned at the level of class and place. At the level of place we have:

(a) *Community of Residence.* All those who are submitted to the same conditions of housing form a community of dwelling. A certain number of common points connect those who, for example, live in maids' rooms on the sixth floor.

(b) *Community of Subsistence.* Recognized businessmen, qualified artisans, etc., draw the inhabitants of the neighborhood to the same meeting places.

The level of class includes:

(a) *Community of Work.* This is formed by all those who do the same kind of work outside or inside the neighborhood, and who can be assembled by the same centers of professional interest.

(b) *Community of Leisure.* The young people meet again in the same cafés and at the same street corners. Movies, squares and beaches are so many assembly points which group the inhabitants by categories of affinity.

2. Elements of a Solution

As a consequence of what we have just said, concerning class, it is necessary to:

(a) locate these human distances;

(b) create bonds between the people making up these communities of destiny to create neighborhood communities;

(c) arouse responsible people capable of taking charge of the neighborhood communities.

Concerning place, it is necessary to define the natural islands. It seems necessary to bring the topography of districts to light to find the streets that divide and join. Sometimes a street itself has a character. Sometimes the two sidewalks of a street are utterly different.

3. The Mainsprings of the Mission

The role of the neighborhood mission is to create human communities of place and class. It should be animated by teams of neighborhood couples, stimulated by chaplains and supported by unmarried lay people.

(a) *Home Teams.* It seems hopeful that the principal workers of the neighborhood mission might be recruited from among the most dynamic, if not necessarily the youngest, couples of the parish. Why couples instead of unmarried people? There is obviously no discrimination according to principle. If we are aware of the psychology of the world of unbelief, we will admit that the witness of young couples is more acceptable than that of unmarried people. Not that the unmarried are less valuable, but the married lay people, because of their family situation, share the condition of life common to the majority of people.

Young responsible couples should group themselves into teams by natural affinities. It is the team which is responsible for this "island," for this community of destiny. A couple responsible for all the teams supervises the group. These teams have the right to take the initiative. It is up to them to organize the mission as they envisage it in their sector, without the chaplain's pressure or precise orders as to the means of practical action.

In these teams, men and women have distinct roles. The man, consecrating the largest part of his time to his profession, has a relatively limited neighborhood life. His professional life enables him to exercise his missionary role at the place of work. In the communities of destiny in his neighborhood, he fills his missionary role in bringing together those who share the same professional interests. Thus, several men exercising the same profession might meet, not to form a supplementary team of people with the same type of job, but with the sole aim of looking for the means to enter into contact with unbelievers who have the same work preoccupations.

The engagement of the man according to that double dimension of place and class makes him able to understand the missionary role of his wife. A woman is expected to be primarily a presence. Her primary role is contact. She belongs naturally to the neighborhood because of her family responsibilities. There she shares the daily life and is attentive to events and the people she meets.

Thus, husbands and wives, while filling a distinct missionary role, can be reciprocally interested in their personal action, have their cares in common and help to resolve the difficulties met in the mission.

(b) *The Priest's Role.* It is important that priests not be the leaders of the teams. The work of the mission would be false if the priest took on all the initiatives and organized the action to be taken in the neighborhood. Unfortunately, this is what happens almost everywhere.

The priest is there to stress the evangelical exigencies, to animate, stimulate and take part in the activities of the mission. This obviously implies a community of work and action between priests. In their meeting with the unbeliever, lay people should be concerned to prepare or encourage the personal contact with them sought by the priest; this is the essential role of the priest. But that does not mean that the role of lay people is reduced to that of forerunner. They have an irreplaceable role. In the dialogue, for example, they can establish a human contact which the priest cannot.

(c) *Unmarried People.* To the extent that unmarried people become integrated into society, assuming their unmarried state, they can assume a radiance from the missionary point of view. The unbeliever should not judge the missionary activity of the unmarried as "compensation." The unbeliever is spontaneously tempted to think that the availability of the unmarried person is the expression of a disability in existence much more than an engagement in life.

By his personal values and his courageous comportment in life, the unmarried person has the grace to bear a specific witness. He is the witness, through the questioning which he provokes in the unbeliever, of a state of life which can only be understood if God exists, if God alone suffices.

If the Christian *couple* bear witness of their attachment to God, it is through the mediation of conjugal love that this witness is perceptible. If the *priest* or *religious* bears witness of a total gift to God, it is through the mediation of the priesthood and the spiritual paternity that this witness of exclusive attachment is perceptible. But if the *unmarried person* bears witness of a real attachment to God, it is through an unselfish love for others. Therefore, it is important that the unmarried person effectively bear this clear witness at the risk of bearing a counter-witness.

From a practical point of view, the missionary role of the unmarried person should be accomplished in a spirit of service. It will often consist of visiting homes, aiding priests in conducting investigations, and recording censuses.

4. Means of Action

(a) *Contacts and Visits.* Contacts should be natural. The systematic door-to-door method is a formal counter-indication. Too many peddlers haunt buildings for the unannounced to be favorably accepted. The missionary, in this case, would only be regarded as a news-vendor sent by the pastor.

The visits made by missionaries should be motivated and purposeful. On the occasion of a family event—birth or death—the contact should be spontaneously established. An event in parochial life—a Church bazaar, for example—can be the occasion for visits which will perhaps be the beginning of a deeper dialogue.

These "occasional" visits can be so in a systematic way: for example, on the occasion of an anniversary. Why not pay a visit one year after the baptism of a baby, the death of a parent, etc., and on that occasion make a gesture of sympathy which is at the same time a witness of faith? To show indifferent parents that the baptism of their baby was remembered one year later proves the seriousness with which the Church has accepted their engagement.

These occasional visits should never be *official visits.* The missionaries who contact the people in the neighborhood should not be considered as licensed visitors of the parish. To visit people demands a comprehension of situation and comportment; it also demands a sense of the opportune moment, presentation, etc.

We do not pay a visit to bring our wealth, but to teach others how to discover the wealth revealed in everything that exists. The attitude of listening and welcoming is obviously primordial. This sense of contact should not, however, lead to avoiding difficult questions which might provoke, on the level of faith, a true encounter. We must know how to approach difficult questions and to help unbelievers understand Christian exigencies.

Thus, for instance, in the matter of the sacraments, it is necessary to explain that the Church might have to refuse a religious burial or an admission to baptism. The unbelievers must be led to understand that such an attitude of the Church reveals the respect that it has for him.

For these visits to be fruitful from the missionary viewpoint, they should be reviewed by the teams to examine what they reveal of the unbeliever's mentality and not remain at the anecdotal stage of the encounter.

Furthermore, it is not a question of simply multiplying contacts; it is necessary to know how to use them to establish a valid missionary dialogue. In this respect, it would be worthwhile if all the teams in the mission brought their efforts to a precise point of common research (for example: How do parents react when they are reminded of the anniversary of their child's baptism?).

(b) *Neighborhood Engagement and Life.* The interest shown by the Christian community in the daily life of the neighborhood will perhaps be interpreted by the unbeliever not only as a mark of sympathy but as the expression of an incarnate charity. It is important, in this case, to be detached from politics or particular interests so that the evangelical spirit appears as the fundamental motive of the action. The engagement of Christians of the community in a household management committee of the 5th and 6th districts of Paris, for example, is registered in this perspective.

(c) *The Place of Neighborhood Events.* The parish newspaper seems to be the most appropriate means of reflecting the life of the neighborhood in its events. It is necessary that it relate these events faithfully and that it know how to take part. The newspaper has an educational role in the matter of judgment; it can be a Christian presence which predisposes the reader to open himself to the Gospel.

How should it be distributed? It does not seem desirable to do so anonymously and without cost because, in this case, it is imposed as publicity and perhaps considered paternalistic. In all contacts with the unbeliever, a free and consented reception should be encouraged. A gesture of participation must be solicited so as not to have the unbeliever set in a passive attitude.

(d) *Opening to the World.* If the missionary must be very attentive to the concrete and immediate realities of the neighborhood, he must at the same time be careful to lead people beyond their own preoccupations in order to open themselves to those of the world. It is essential that the missionary help them judge the events which mark worldly reality and which influence mentalities. What we at Saint-Severin call the "concern of the month" should be conceived of in terms of the inhabitants of the neighborhood so that, on the occasion of an event concerning the whole world, there might be a possible local terrain for dialogue.

5. Manifestations of the Christian Community

(a) *Its Educational Institutions of Faith.* The catechumenate for adults has an important role, for its reason for being is the opening to the faith and its development. It is not enough to enter into contact with the unbeliever; he must be welcomed and furnished with the means for informing and cultivating himself and believing.

Catechism classes create a privileged terrain which situates the dialogue without the ambiguity which can be had with non-Christian parents. If all the adults engaged in the religious classes of childhood were concerned with a missionary contact with the parents, the catechism would represent one of the primary missionary activities in the parish.

(b) *Its Permanent Services.* Welcome, mutual aid, corporal works of mercy, lunches for old people, dispensary, social service, youth movements—these are all signs which reveal the desire of the Christian community to be present in a concrete and unselfish way. The value of these institutions is conditioned by the missionary spirit animating them; their criterion is the quality of the contacts provoked by them.

(c) *Its Festivities.* To the extent that festivities permit those we call "marginal" to integrate with the Christian community, it can be said that they have a missionary importance. In the same way, to the extent that festivities evoke a sympathetic feeling from the "indifferent" of the neighborhood, they are of pre-missionary value.

III
CONCLUSION

The mission is not improvised. The mission should be effective. The concern for missionary efficiency is proof of good health, psychological as well as spiritual.

The mission demands competence. Empiricists, busybodies, dilettantes and the "unemployed" of parochial works are the counter-missionaries who are unaware of it.

But the mission is not the undertaking of public works of the Church. The way in which we have situated the neighborhood mission in the broad outlines of its practical organization should not make us think that it is reduced to a technique. Contrary to what good parishioners might say, we do not carry on the missions; rather *we are missionaries*.

We have to incessantly exercise our wits to find forms of action suited to the needs of our epoch. At the same time, we must remember that the mission is essentially the expression, in acts, of a missionary spirit which is none other than the very Spirit of Christ communicated in his Church.

11 SPIRITUALITY AND MISSION
Peter's Faith and John's Witness

I

SPIRITUAL TESTAMENT OF THE MISSION

Prayer, Love, Humility

Every missionary effort remains unbridled if it is not supported by prayer.

Prayer, through the stripping of spirit it demands, purifies intentions.

Prayer is the criterion of the truth of the mission.

Every missionary engagement is marked with sterility if it is not nourished by a faith full of love. Charity is the seal of the truth of the mission.

Every initiative becomes foolish if it is not rooted in humility.

Humility is the guarantee of the truth of the mission.

Spirit and Spirituality

Embroidery is out of style. Thus, rather than piously unravel edifying repetitions, we will leave to everyone the grace of rediscovering for himself the spirit of all spirituality through the greater life of the prophets and the first apostles.

Two parallel evangelical texts, understood through each other, open at the meditation on Peter's faith and John the Baptist's witness. They recall, if such is necessary, that the spirituality of the mission is not an elegant way out of the harsh realities of action.

II

PETER'S FAITH

"Now Jesus, having come into the district of Caesarea Philippi, began to ask his disciples, saying, 'Who do men say the Son of Man is?' But they said, 'Some say John the Baptist; and others, Elias and others Jeremiah, or one of the prophets.' He said to them, 'But who do you say that I am?' Simon Peter answered and said, 'Thou art the Christ, the Son of the living God.' Then Jesus answered and said, 'Blessed art thou, Simon Bar-Jona, for flesh and blood has not revealed this to thee, but my Father in heaven. And I say to thee, thou art Peter, and upon this rock I will build my Church, and the gates of hell shall not prevail against it. And I will give thee the keys of the kingdom of heaven; and whatever thou shalt bind on earth should be bound in heaven, and whatever thou shalt loose on earth shall be loosed in heaven' " (Matthew 16, 13-19).

1. *"Art Thou Then the Son of God?"* (Lk. 22, 70)

"Who do men say that I am?" Would that be a question of reputation?

Would Christ be preoccupied with his fame to the point of wishing to know what people thought about him?

It would really be necessary not to know that God is God and to be completely ignorant of the Gospel to founder in such low contempt.

Anyone familiar with the Gospel is not surprised at the question. It is the question of confidence *par excellence,* because it is the unique question of faith.

In St. Mark, the "evangelist of the messianic secret"—so called for having centered the composition of his gospel on the divinity of Christ—that question is found at the summit of his work; it is the ultimate question, the stumbling block.[1] *"Who do you say that I am?"*

Putting the question to the circle of the disciples once more, Christ urges them to be conscious of the contents of their faith's

---

[1] In St. Mark, Peter's profession of faith is found in Chapter 8. There are 16 chapters in this gospel.

adherence. He asks them this question to lead them to express their opinion of his person and, through that, to help them to be further introduced into his mystery as the Son of God.

This is the teaching of Christ which the Church extends. At baptism, doesn't the child—in the person of the privileged witnesses who are the godparents—begin by declaring himself for Jesus Christ, Son of God? Afterward, throughout his life, he will discover it personally in a growing and perfectible faith. Whoever seeks God discovers him in declaring himself for Jesus Christ, Son of God. Such was the way of Peter.

"Thou art the Christ, the Son of the Living God." Religion, as P. Loew has said, consists of "being bound anew to God." [2] Faith is the sort of knowledge which engages. It is defined by the capacity, greater or smaller according to each one, to recognize in Jesus Christ the Son of God.

The religious Jews, who took Christ for one of the prophets— John the Baptist, Elias, Jeremiah—scorned him. In the strictest sense of the term, they did not have faith. They made the same error as the Moslems who consider Christ to be the greatest of the prophets.

Peter, who had discerned in Christ the person of the Son of God, adhered to him in this total faith as Christ desired it, conscious and lucid. Christ, sent by the Father to reveal "truth in its fullness," leads us by the Spirit to total faith.[3]

By total faith we mean that movement of adhering which seizes its object in its entirety. He is totally believing who, within the limits of the mystery but with full knowledge of its limits, adheres completely to the entire revelation.

Theologians can still discuss for a long time whether the first apostles, in their profession of faith at Caesarea, grasped what we perceive ourselves today. It is not very likely that Peter put all the theological contents which we can find into an affirmation which centuries of faith have not finished studying thoroughly. But that is not important. His faith was integral; Jesus himself declared him blessed for having recognized him, not because of the knowledge which he could have by himself, but because of the knowledge which the Father communicated to him. The Church transmits this

---

[2] *Si vous saviez le don de Dieu,* p. 8.
[3] "But when he, the Spirit of truth, has come, he will teach you all the truth" (Jn. 16, 13).

grace to us. It remains for us, by means of a lucid and intelligent adherence of faith, to spread it.

2. *"Blessed Are Your Eyes, For They See"* (Mt. 13, 16)

Jesus wants to know himself the way in which the revelation is understood. Even with the message announced, he does not consider his mission accomplished. He is not content to cast the Good News to the winds, but is concerned to know if it is received by all.

(a) *He Provokes Reactions.* Many times, he publicly arouses adherence to the faith. We recall, at the resurrection of Lazarus, Martha's profession of faith, comparable to that of Peter:

" 'Whoever lives and believes in me shall never die. Dost thou believe this?' She said to him, 'Yes, Lord, I believe that thou art the Christ, the Son of God, who hast come into the world' " (Jn. 11, 26-27).

(b) *He Probes Opinion.* "Who do men say that I am?" These are the people who interest him, the unimportant people; not the scientists and intellectuals, but those whom we, with the psalmist, have already called "common people":

"I praise thee, Father, Lord of heaven and earth, that thou didst hide these things from the wise and prudent, and didst reveal them to little ones" (Mt. 11, 25).

(c) *He Involves His Life in the Question He Asks.* It is only a short time before his death, at the moment he officially announces his passion, that Christ asks this question about his person. It is a crucial moment on which his existence depends, a privileged moment which permits his disciples to understand the meaning of the question in grasping the meaning of his life. The missionary can ask that question of God from the instant it appears, for it is the question which engages his existence and gives all meaning to his human life. The meaning of life, as Christ revealed it, is love. That is why Christ cannot reveal *who* he is without declaring: "The world [must] know that I love the Father" (Jn. 14, 31).

The world must also know that I, as Christ's disciple, confront myself with God's mystery because I love him. The world will discover that love through the personal relation which binds me to God and which is confirmed in the mission I receive from him by the engagement of baptism. Every profession of faith is extended by the mission and authenticated by the engagement which it implies.

Peter declared: "Thou art the Christ, the Son of the living God." The Lord takes him at his word: "Thou art Peter, and upon this rock I will build my Church." "Lord, thou knowest well that I love thee," says Peter after the resurrection, and the Lord reflects that declaration of love in the mission which he confides to him: "Feed my lambs" (Jn. 21, 16).

I declared on the day of my baptism: "I believe in Jesus Christ, the only Son of the Father." The Lord takes me in his Word. This Word binds me and I understand: "You are a rock in my Church; by this rock and with all others, I will build the world that it may become the Church."

In this mutual engagement which binds man to the Son of God, the question which emerges definitively is one which Christ could have put in these terms: "Are you ready, *because of me,* to become what I myself, *because of you,* have become, the mediator between God and men?"

It is in this personal relation, made clear by the insistence with which Christ underlined the "because of me" of the Gospel, that the mediation of love, which is the final word of the mission, is realized.[4]

III

JOHN'S WITNESS

"This is the witness of John, when the Jews sent to him from Jerusalem priests and Levites to ask him 'Who art thou?' And he acknowledged and did not deny; and he acknowledged, 'I am not the Christ.' And they asked him, 'What then. Art thou Elias?' And he said, 'I am not.' 'Art thou the Prophet?' And he answered, 'No.'

"They therefore said to him, 'Who art thou, that we may give an answer to those who sent us? What has thou to say of thyself?' He said, 'I am the voice of one crying in the desert, "Make straight the way of the Lord," as said Isaiah the prophet.'

"And they who had been sent were from among the Pharisees. And they asked him and said to him, 'Why, then, dost thou bap-

---

[4] "He who finds his life will lose it, and he who loses his life for my sake will find it" (Mt. 10, 39). "Blessed are you when men reproach you, and persecute you, and, speaking falsely, say all manner of evil against you, for my sake" (Mt. 5, 11).

tize, if thou art not the Christ, nor Elias, nor the Prophet?' John said
to them in answer: 'I baptize with water; but in the midst of you
there has stood one whom you do not know. He it is who is to
come after me, who has been set above me, the strap of whose
sandal I am not worthy to loose.'

"These things took place at Bethany, beyond the Jordan, where
John was baptizing" (Jn. 1, 19-28).

1. *"No Servant Is Greater Than His Master"* (Jn. 15, 20)

Christ had asked: "Who do men say that I am?" The question is
now reversed. These are the people themselves who had called the
witness to account: "Who are you?"

The scorn is prolonged and aggravated. Whereas Christ is confused with one of the prophets, John is taken for *the* prophet, the
Messiah. The substitution is serious. To confuse the witness with
the one to whom witness is rendered is to condemn that witness,
to fail to recognize him and, finally, to reject him.

The suffering of the witness is not so much in being rejected as
in reliving the rejection of Christ: "Let not my unprovoked enemies rejoice over me" (Ps. 35, 19). Christ is not spoken of without impunity. Credentials must be shown in the full knowledge that
they will be refused.

When he is taken for another, when he is accused of intentions
he does not have, when what he says is twisted, when he is mis-
trusted, the only strength left to the witness is the love which gives
him further courage to say "no" to all that distorts his witness.

2. *"Let Your 'No' Mean 'No'"* (Mt. 5, 37)

Let it mean "no" to error and to the hypocrisy of those who
would like to annex the witness to justify their good conscience.

Let it mean "no" to the passivity of those who nourish themselves with the illusion of faith and who grimace at four stages in
their life: baptism, communion, marriage and death.

Let it mean "no" to caricatures of a message lowered to the
mediocrity of those of whom demands are no longer made.

Let it mean "no" to profiteers who use the Church like a gold mine without making the least sign of opening to her mystery.

Let us say "yes" to the truth.

3. *"Who Art Thou, That We May Give an Answer . . ."*

(a) *Witness Is Transparency.* It is not for me, the witness, to ask the question of the person of Jesus Christ, Son of God, but for God. Only God may ask "Who am I?" God asks this question through me, through the language of love which I love. Since "it is not I who live, but Christ in me," that love which identifies the Christian with Christ must be recognized as that by the unbeliever. It is thus in asking the Witness "Who are you?" that the unbeliever can perhaps discover that the only response is Christ's question which challenges directly: "For you, who am I?"

(b) *Witness Is a Passing Over.* The Gospel would say that the witness is a useless servant—a useless servant, but indispensable.

Useless, for he knows very well that it is not he who passes over but the Lord. Nothing serves as passage if the Lord does not pass over.

Useless, for only Christ is the way: "Without me you can do nothing" (Jn. 15, 5).

Indispensable, because the passage is one with the way. The way would be impracticable without passage. The witness is one through whom the Lord indicates the way: "Every valley shall be filled in, every mountain and hill shall be made low; the rugged land shall be made a plain, the rough country, a broad valley. Then the glory of the Lord shall be revealed, and all mankind shall see it together" (Is. 40, 4-5).

Indispensable, since it is he who opens the way, crying in the desert—in the world and not in a void: "Prepare the way of the Lord! Make straight in the wasteland a highway for our God" (Is. 40, 3).

Indispensable, for the witness is the guide who indicates the direction of the road: "In the midst of you there has stood one whom you do not know" (Jn. 1, 26).

To accept the link between the foolish and the indispensable, in the faith's stripping of self, is to consent to take, in hope, the way of the mission.

Suggested Readings

Abbott, Walter M. (ed.), *The Documents of Vatican II*. New York, Guild Press/Association Press.

Alexander, Calvert, *The Missionary Dimension of the Church*. Milwaukee, Bruce Publishing Co.

Burns, Patrick J. (ed.), *Mission and Witness*. Westminster, Md., Newman Press.

Chenu, M.-D., *Theology of Work*. Chicago, Henry Regnery Co.

Congar, Yves, *Lay People in the Church*. Newman Press.

De Smedt, Bishop Emile-Joseph, *The Priesthood of the Faithful*. Glen Rock, N.J., Paulist Press.

Hastings, Adrian, *The Church's No. 1 Problem: Mission*. Paulist Press (pamphlet).

Michonneau, G., *The Missionary Spirit in Parish Life*. Newman Press; *Revolution in a City Parish*. Newman Press; with R. Meurice, *Catholic Action and the Parish*. Newman Press.

Paul VI, Encyclical *Ecclesiam Suam*. Paulist Press.

Rahner, Karl, *Christian in the Marketplace*. New York, Sheed & Ward; *Free Speech in the Church*, Sheed & Ward; *Hearers of the World*, New York, Herder & Herder; *Theology for Renewal: Bishops, Priests, Laity*. Herder & Herder.

Rétif, André and Louis, *The Church's Mission in the World*. Paulist Press.

Sheerin, John B., Commentary on the *Decree on the Apostolate of the Laity*. Paulist Press.

Sheppard, Lancelot C., *Charles de Foucauld*. Dublin, Clonmore and Reynolds.

Suhard, Emmanuel, *The Church Today*. Chicago, Fides; *Priests among Men: Growth or Decline*. Fides.